AF316663

THE PERSON OF CHRIST

THE MIRACLE OF HISTORY

PHILIP SCHAFF

PREFATORY MATERIAL

"WHAT do ye think of the Son of Man?" This is the religious question of the age. We rejoice in it, and thank the infidel biographers of Jesus for having urged it upon the attention of the world. The result of the renewed struggle can not be doubtful: in all theological controversies, truth is the gainer in the end. Though nailed to the cross, and buried in the tomb, it rises again triumphant over error, taking captivity captive, and changing at times even a bitter foe, like Saul of Tarsus, into a devoted friend. Goethe says: "The conflict of faith and unbelief remains the proper, the only, the deepest theme of the history of the world and mankind, to which all others are subordinated." This very conflict centers in the Christological problem.

The question of Christ is the question of Christianity, which is the manifestation of his life in the world; it is the question of the Church, which rests upon him as the immovable rock; it is the question of history, which revolves around him as the central sun of the moral universe; it is the question of every man, who instinctively yearns after him as the object of his noblest and purest aspirations; it is a question of personal salvation, which can only be obtained in the blessed name of Jesus. The whole fabric of Christianity stands or falls with its divine-human Founder; and if it can never perish, it is because Christ lives, the same yesterday, to-day, and for ever.

The object of this book is simply to show, in a popular style, that the Person of Christ is the great central miracle of history, and the strongest evidence of Christianity. The very perfection of his humanity is a proof of his Divinity. The indwelling of God in him is the only satisfactory solution of the problem of his amazing character.

From his miraculous Person, his miraculous works follow as an inevitable consequence. Being a miracle himself, he must perform miracles with the same ease with which ordinary men do their ordinary works. The contrary would be unnatural. The character of the tree determines the nature of the fruit. "Believe me that I am in the Father, and the Father in me; *or else* believe me for the very works' sake" (John xiv. 11; comp. x. 38). I believe in Christ, and *therefore* I believe the Bible, and all its wonderful words and wonderful works.

Standing on this rock, I feel safe against all the attacks of infidelity. The person of Christ is to me the greatest and surest of all facts; as certain as my own personal existence; yea, even more so: for Christ lives in me, and he is the only valuable part of my being. I am nothing without my Saviour. I am all with him, and would not exchange him for ten thousand worlds. To give up faith in Christ is to give up faith in humanity. Such skepticism legitimately ends at last in the nihilism of despair.

This volume has grown out of an essay of the author, on the *Moral Character of Christ*, originally prepared for the Porter Rhetorical Society, of the Theological Seminary at Andover, Mass., and delivered at its anniversary, Aug. 1, 1860.[1] The *Collection of Testimonies of Unbelievers* to the moral perfection of Christ, is, to my knowledge, the first attempt of the kind, and hence far from being complete. But all our works are mere fragments.

Infidels are seldom convinced by argument; for the springs of unbelief are in the heart rather than in the head. But honest inquirers and earnest skeptics, like Nathanael and Thomas, who love the truth, and wish only for tangible support of their weak faith, will never refuse, when the evidence is laid before them, to embrace it with grateful joy, and to worship the incarnate God. Blessed are they that seek the truth; for they shall find it.

P. S.

Bible House, New York,

May 11, 1865.

---

1. The original title is: *The Moral Character of Christ; or, The Perfection of Christ's Humanity a Proof of his Divinity. A Theological Tract for the People*. The essay was first published as an article in the *Mercersburg Review*, Chambersburg, Penn., 1861, pp. 53; and twice republished in England, in the *British and Foreign Evangelical Review*, and by the London Religious Tract Society, 1863. It is referred to repeatedly in the seventh edition of Dr. Ullmaun's book on the Sinlessness of Jesus, as also in Dr. Dorner's essay on the same subject.

WHEN the angel of the Lord appeared to Moses in the burning bush, he was commanded to put off his shoes from his feet; for the place whereon he stood was holy ground. With what reverence and awe, then, should we approach the contemplation of the great reality—God manifest in the flesh—of which the vision of Moses was but a significant type and shadow![1]

The life and character of Jesus Christ is truly the holy of holies in the history of the world. Eighteen hundred years have passed away since he appeared, in the fullness of time, on this earth to redeem a fallen race from sin and death, and to open a never-ceasing fountain of righteousness and life. The ages before him anxiously awaited his coming, as the fulfillment of the desire of all nations: the ages after him proclaim his glory, and ever extend his dominion. The noblest and best of men under every clime hold him not only in the purest affection and the profoundest gratitude, but in divine adoration and worship. His name is above every name that may be named in heaven or on earth, and the only one whereby the sinner can be saved. He is the Author of the new creation; the Way, the Truth, and the Life; the Prophet, Priest, and King of regenerate humanity. He is Immanuel, God with us; the Eternal Word become flesh; very God and very man in one undivided person, the Saviour of the world.

Thus he stands out to the faith of the entire Christian Church—Greek, Latin, and Evangelical—in every civilized country on the globe. Much as the various confessions and denominations differ in doctrines and usages, they are agreed in their love and adoration of Jesus. They lay down their arms when they approach the manger of Bethlehem or the cross of Calvary, where he was born and died for our sins that we might live for ever in heaven. He is the divine harmony of all human sects and creeds, the common life-center of all true Christians; where their hearts meet with their affections, prayers, and hopes, in spite of the discord of their heads in views and theories. The doctrines and institutions, the worship and customs, the sciences and arts, of all Christendom, bear witness to the indelible impression he made upon the world; countless churches and cathedrals are as many monuments of gratitude to his holy name; and thousands of hymns and prayers are daily and hourly ascending to his praise from public and private sanctuaries in all parts of the globe. His power is now greater, his kingdom larger, than ever; and it will continue to spread, until all nations shall bow before him, and kiss his scepter of righteousness and peace.

Blessed is he who from the heart can believe that Jesus is the Son of God, and the fountain of salvation. True faith is indeed no work of nature, but an act of God wrought in the soul by the Holy Ghost, who reveals Christ to us in his true character, as Christ has revealed the Father. Faith, with its justifying, sanctifying, and saving power, is independent of science and learning, and may be kindled even in the heart of a little child and an illiterate slave. It is the peculiar glory of the Redeemer and his religion to be co-extensive with humanity itself, without distinction of sex, age, nation, and race. His saving grace flows and overflows to all and for all, on the simple condition of repentance and faith.

This fact, however, does not supersede the necessity of thought and argument. Revelation, although above nature and above reason, is not against nature or against reason. On the contrary, nature and the supernatural, as has been well said by a distinguished New-England divine, "constitute together the one system of God."[2] Christianity satisfies the deepest intellectual as well as moral and religious wants of man, who is created in the image and for the glory of God. It is the revelation of truth as well as of life. Faith and knowledge, pistis and gnosis, are not antagonistic, but complementary forces; not enemies, but inseparable twin-sisters. Faith precedes knowledge, but just as necessarily leads to knowledge; while true knowledge, on the other hand, is always rooted and grounded in faith, and tends to confirm and to strengthen it. Thus we find the two combined in the famous confession of Peter, when he says, in the name of all the other apostles, "We *believe* and we *know* that thou art Christ."[3] So intimately are both connected, that we may also reverse the famous maxim of Augustine, Anselm, and Schleiermacher: "Faith precedes knowledge,"[4] and say: "Knowledge precedes faith."[5] For how can we believe in any object without at least some general historical knowledge of its existence and character? Faith even in its first form, as a submission to the authority of God and an assent to the truth of his revelation, is an exercise of the mind and reason as well as of the heart and the will. Hence faith has been defined as implying three things,—knowledge, assent, and trust or confidence. An idiot or a madman can not believe. Our religion demands not a blind, but a rational, intelligent faith; and this just in proportion to its strength and fervor, aims at an ever-deepening insight into its own sacred contents and object.

As living faith in Christ is the soul and center of all sound practical Christianity and piety, so the true doctrine of Christ is the soul and center of all sound Christian theology. St. John makes the denial of the incarnation of the Son of God the criterion of Antichrist, and consequently the belief in this central truth the test of Christianity. The incarnation of the eternal Logos, and the divine glory shining through the veil of Christ's humanity, is the grand theme of his Gospel, which he wrote with the pen of an angel from the very heart of Christ, as his favorite disciple and bosom-friend. The Apostles' Creed, starting as it does from the confession of Peter, makes the article on Christ most prominent, and assigns to it the central position between the preceding article on God the Father, and the succeeding article on the Holy Ghost. The development of ancient Catholic theology commenced and culminated with the triumphant defense of the true divinity, and true humanity of Christ, against the opposite heresies of Judaizing Ebionism, which denied the former, and paganizing Gnosticism, which resolved the latter into a shadowy phantom. The evangelical Protestant theology, in its sound form, is essentially Christological, or controlled throughout by the proper idea of Christ as the God-Man and Saviour. This is emphatically the article of the standing or falling Church. In this, the two most prominent ideas of the Reformation—the doctrine of the supremacy of the Scriptures, and the doctrine of justification by grace through faith—meet, and are vitally united. Christ's word, the only unerring and efficient guide of truth; Christ's work, the only unfailing and sufficient source of peace; Christ all in all,—this is the principle of genuine Protestantism.

In the construction of the true doctrine of Christ's person, we may, with St. John in the prologue to his Gospel, begin from above with his eternal Godhead, and proceed, through the creation and the preparatory revelation of the Old Testament economy, till we reach the incarnation and his truly human life for the redemption of the race. Or, with the other evangelists, we may begin from below with his birth from the Virgin Mary, and rise, through the successive stages of his earthly life, his discourses and miracles, to his assumption into that divine glory which he had before the foundation of the world. The result reached in both cases is the same; namely, that Christ unites in his person the whole fullness of the Godhead, and the whole fullness of sinless manhood.

The older theologians, both Catholic and Evangelical, proved the divinity of the Saviour in a direct way from the *miracles* performed by him; from the *prophecies* and *types* fulfilled in him; from the divine *names* which he bears; from the divine *attributes* which are predicated of him; from the divine *works* which he performed; and from the divine *honors* which he claims, and which are fully accorded to him by his apostles and the whole Christian Church to this day.

But it may also be proved by the opposite process,—the contemplation of the singular perfection of Christ's humanity; which rises by almost universal consent, even of unbelievers, so far above every human greatness known before or since, that it can only be rationally explained on the ground of such an essential union with the Godhead as he claimed himself, and as his inspired apostles ascribed to him. The more deeply we penetrate the veil of his flesh, the more clearly we behold the glory of the Only-Begotten of the Father shining through the same, full of grace and of truth.[6]

Modern evangelical theology owes this new homage to the Saviour. The powerful and subtle attacks of the latest phases of infidelity upon the credibility of the gospel history call for a more vigorous defense than was ever made before, and have already led, by way of re-action, to new triumphs of the old faith of the Church in her divine Head.

Our humanitarian, philanthropic, and yet skeptical age is more susceptible to this argument, which proceeds from the humanity to the divinity, than the old dogmatic method of demonstration which follows the opposite process. With Thomas, the representative of honest and earnest skepticism among the apostles, many noble and inquiring minds refuse to believe in the divinity of the Lord, unless supported by the testimony of their senses, or the convincing arguments of reason: they desire to put the finger into the print of his nails, and to thrust the hand into his side, before they exclaim, in humble adoration: "My Lord and my God!" They can not easily he brought to believe in miracles on abstract reasoning or on historical evidence. But, if they once could see the great moral miracle of Christ's person and character, they would have no difficulty with the miracles of his works. For a superhuman being must of necessity do superhuman deeds; a miraculous person must perform miraculous works. The contrary would be unnatural, and the greatest miracle. The character of the tree accounts for the character of the fruit. We believe in the miracles of Christ because we believe in his person as the divine Man, and the central miracle of the moral universe.

It is from this point of view that we shall endeavor, in as popular and concise a manner as the difficulty and dignity of the subject permit, to analyze and exhibit the *human character* of Christ. We propose to take up the man, Jesus of Nazareth, as he appears on the simple, unsophisticated record of the plain and honest fishermen of Galilee, and as he lives in the faith of Christendom; and we shall find him in all the stages of his life, both as a private individual and as a public character, so far elevated above the reach of successful rivalry, and so singularly perfect, that this very perfection, in the midst of an imperfect and sinful world, constitutes an irresistible proof of his divinity.

A full discussion of the subject would require us to consider Christ in his official as well as personal character; and to describe him as a teacher, a reformer, a worker of miracles, and the founder of a spiritual kingdom universal in extent and. perpetual in time. From every point of view, we should be irresistibly driven to the same result. But our present purpose confines us to the consideration of his personal character; and this alone, we think, is sufficient for the conclusion.

---

1. The painter-monk Fra Beato Angelico da Fiesole (born in Fiesole, near Florence, in 1387, died in Rome in 1455), one of the purest characters in the whole history of art, who from the seraphic beauty of his angels and glorified saints was called "the blessed" and "the angelic," painted the head of Christ and of the holy Virgin always in a praying frame of mind and on his knees. " It would be well for criticism," says E. Renan (in his *"Studies of Religious History and Criticism,"* transl. by O. B. Frothingham, New York, 1864, p. 168), "to imitate his example, and, only after having adored them, to face the radiance of certain figures before which the ages have bent low." Unfortunately, the French philosopher understands this in the sense of pantheistic hero-worship. We regard only one man as worthy of divine honor and worship,—the God-Man, Jesus of Nazareth.

2. See Dr. Horace Bushnell's able work on *"Nature and the Supernatural."* The same idea is expressed by Dr. John W. Nevin, in his book on *"The Mystical Presence,"* Phil., 1846, p. 199, in these words: "Nature and revelation, the world and Christianity, as springing from the same Divine Mind, are not two different systems joined together in a merely outward way. They form a single whole, harmonious with itself in all its parts. The sense of the one, then, is necessarily included and comprehended in the sense of the other. The mystery of the new creation must involve, in the end, the mystery of the old; and the key that serves to unlock the meaning of the first must serve to unlock the inmost secret of the last."

3. John vi. 69: "We have believed and know" (ἡμεῖς πεπιστεύκαμεν καὶ ἐγνώκαμεν, *credidimus et cognovimus*). The reverse order we have in John x. 38: "That ye may know and believe that the Father is in me, and I in him;" and in 1 John v. 13.

4. *Fides præcedit intellectum.* Or more fully, in the language of Anselm of Canterbury, adopted by Schleiermacher as the motto of his Dogmatics: *"Neque enim quæro intelligere ut credam sed credo ut intelligam. Nam qui non crediderit, non experietur, et qui expertus non fuerit, non intelliget."*

5. *Intellectus præcedit fidem.* This was Abelard's maxim, which, without the restriction of the opposite maxim, must lead to rationalism and skepticism.

6. Dr. Ullmann, *"Die Sündlosigkeit Jesu,"* 6th ed. p. 215: *"So führt schon das Vollendet-Menschliche in Jesu, wenn wir es mit allem Uebrigen, was die Menschheit*

darbietet, vergleichen, zur Anerkennung des Göttlichen in ihm." Dorner, *"Entwicklungsgeschichte der Lehre von der Person Christi,"* 2d ed. vol. ii. p. 1211: *"Jesu Heiligkeit und Weisheit, durch die er unter den sündigen, vielirrenden Menschen einzig dasteht, weiset . . . . auf einen übernatürlichen Ursprung seiner Person. Diese muss, um inmitten der Sünderwelt begreiflich zu sein, aus einer eigenthümlichen und wunderbar schöpferischen That Gottes abgeleitet, ja es muss in Christus . . . . von Gott aus betrachtet, eine Incarnation göttlicher Liebe, also göttlichen Wesens gesehen werden, was ihn als den Punkt erscheinen lässt, wo Gott und die Menschheit einzig und innigst geeinigt sind."* Compare also Ebrard, *"Christliche Dogmatik,"* 1852, vol. ii. pp. 24-31; and W. Nast, *"Commentary on Matthew and Mark,"* Cincinnati, 1864, Gener. Introd., pp. 120.

LITERATURE

The literature on the Life and Character of Christ has of late received very large additions in Germany, France, Holland, England, and the United States. We confine ourselves to a list of such books and tracts as treat more immediately of the moral character and sinlessness of Christ, and rise from the contemplation of his perfect humanity to his divinity.

Dr. Carl Ullmann (formerly Professor of Church History in Heidelberg, died Jan. 1865):—*Die Sündlosigkeit Jesu. Eine apologetische Betrachtung* (i.e., *The Sinlessness of Jesus: An Evidence of Christianity*). First published as an article in the German Theological Quarterly Review, *Studien und Kritiken*, for 1828, No. 1; then as a separate book, 6th edition, Heidelberg, 1853; 7th edition, partly rewritten, 1863. (The references to this book in the following tract are partly to the 6th, partly to the 7th, edition.) English translation from the 6th edition by Lundin Brown. Edinburgh: 1858.

Dr. James Waddell Alexander (of New York, died 1859):—*The Character of Jesus: An Argument for the Divine Origin of Christianity.* Published in the *Lectures on the Evidences of Christianity delivered at the University of Virginia.* New York: 1852. pp. 193-211.

John Young:—*The Christ of History: An Argument grounded in the Facts of his Life on Earth.* London: Republished in New York, 1858.

Dr. Horace Bushnell (of Hartford):—*The Character of Jesus forbidding His Classification with Men.* New York: 1861. (Originally the tenth chapter of his very able and interesting work, *Nature and the Supernatural, as together constituting the one System of God.* New York: 1858. pp. 276-299.)

Peter Bayne (M. A., of Scotland):—*The Testimony of Christ to Christianity.* Republished in Boston, 1862.

Dr. Isaac Dorner (Professor of Theology at Berlin):—*On the Sinless Perfection of Jesus* (*Ueber Jesu sündlose Vollkommenheit*), in the Annals of German Theology. Gotha, vol. vii. 1862, pp. 49-106; and in pamphlet form. Also translated into French for the *Revue Chrétienne*, and into English by Prof. Dr. Henry B. Smith for the American Presbyterian Review. New York: 1863.

Dr. J. J. van Oosterzee (Professor of Theology at Utrecht):—*Das Bild Christi nach der Schrift.* Hamburg: 1864. (*The Image of Christ according to the Scriptures.*) Translated from the Dutch by F. Meyeringh. It is the third part of a larger work of the author, published at Rotterdam, 1855-1861, in three parts,—part first treating of the Christology of the Old Testament, part second of the Christology of the New Testament, part third stating the results, and forming a complete work by itself. It describes the Son of God before his incarnation, the Son of God in the flesh, and the Son of God in glory.

Two French works, which seem to follow the same train of thought, I know only by name: E. Dandiran: *Essai sur la divinité du charactère moral de Jésus-Christ.* Genève: 1850. And Edm. de Pressensé:—*Le Rédempteur.* Paris: 1854. (Recently translated into English.) I also direct attention to M. Guizot:—*Méditations sur l'essence de la religion chrétienne.* Première série. Paris and Leipzig: 1864. The 8th Meditation, pp. 251-329, treats of Christ according to the Gospels.

For older works on the sinless character of Christ, see Ullmann's book above quoted, pp. 231-240 of the seventh edition.

To this list may be added the works on the *Life of Christ* by Hase, Neander, Lange (whose full and comprehensive Life of the Lord Jesus Christ has just been translated and published in Scotland in six vols., Edinburgh, 1864), Ebrard, Sepp (R. C.), Kuhn (R. C.), Lichtenstein, Ewald, Riggenbach, Baumgarten, Ellicott, Andrews; and the very numerous apologetic replies to the infidel *Leben Jesu* of D. F. Strauss, and the *Vie de Jésus* of E. Renan, both of which have indirectly done great service to truth by inviting new and more thorough investigation of the gospel history in all its parts. Reference will be made to them in the course of our discussion, especially at the close.

THE PERSON OF CHRIST

1

HIS CHILDHOOD AND YOUTH

CHRIST passed through all the stages of human life from infancy to manhood, and represented each in its ideal form, that he might redeem and sanctify them all, and be a perpetual model for imitation. He was the model infant, the model boy, the model youth, and the model man.[1] But the weakness, decline, and decrepitude of old age would be incompatible with his character and mission. He died and rose in the full bloom of early manhood, and lives in the hearts of his people in unfading freshness and unbroken vigor for ever.

Let us first glance at the INFANCY and CHILDHOOD of our Saviour. The history of the race commences with the beauty of innocent youth in the garden of Eden, "when the morning stars sang together, and all the sons of God shouted for joy," in beholding Adam and Eve created in the image of their Maker,—the crowning glory of all his wonderful works. So the second Adam, the Redeemer of the fallen race, the Restorer and Perfecter of man, comes first before us in the accounts of the Gospels as a child, born, not in Paradise, it is true, but among the dreary ruins of sin and death; from an humble virgin, in a lowly manger, yet pure and innocent,—the subject of the praise of angels, and the adoration of men. Even the announcement and expectation of his birth transforms his virgin mother, the bride of the humble carpenter, into an inspired prophetess and poetess; rejuvenates the aged parents of the Baptist in hopeful anticipation of the approaching salvation; and makes the unborn babe leap in Elizabeth's womb,—the babe who was to prepare the way for his coming. The immortal psalms of Elizabeth, Mary, and Zacharias, combine the irresistible charms of poetry with truth, and are a worthy preparation for the actual appearance of the Christ-child, at the very threshold of the gospel salvation, when the highest poetry was to become reality, and reality to surpass the sublimest ideal of poetry.[2] And, when the heavenly child was born, heaven and earth, the shepherds of Bethlehem in the name of Israel longing after salvation, and the wise men from the East as the representatives of heathenism in its dark groping after the "unknown God," unite in the worship of the infant King and Saviour.

Here we meet, at the very beginning of the earthly history of Christ, that singular combination of humility and grandeur, of simplicity and sublimity, of the human and divine, which characterizes it throughout, and distinguishes it from every other history. He appears ill the world first as a child, as a poor child, in one of the smallest towns of a remote country,[3] in one of the lowliest spots of that town, in a stable, in a manger, a helpless fugitive from the wrath of a cruel tyrant,—thus presenting, at first sight, every stumbling-block to our faith. But, on the other hand, the appearance of the angel; the inspired hymns of Zacharias and Mary; the holy exultation of Elizabeth, Hannah, and Simeon; the prophecies of Scripture; the theological lore of the scribes at Jerusalem; even the dark political suspicion of Herod; the star of Bethlehem; the journey of the magi from the distant East; the dim light of astrology; the significant night-vision of Joseph; and God's providence overruling every event,—form a glorious array of evidences for the divine origin of the Christ-child; and heaven and earth seem to move around him as their center, which repels whatever is dark and evil, and by the same power attracts what is good and noble. What a contrast! A child in the manger, yet hearing the salvation of the world; a child hated and feared, yet longed for and loved; a child poor and despised, yet honored and adored,—beset by danger, yet marvelously preserved; a child setting the stars in heaven, the city of Jerusalem, the shepherds of Judea, and the sages of the East, in motion,

—attracting the best elements of the world, and repelling the evil! This contrast, bringing together the most opposite yet not contradictory things, is too deep, too sublime, too significant, to be the invention of a few illiterate fishermen.[4]

Yet, with all these marks of divinity upon him, the infant Saviour is not represented, either by Matthew or Luke, as an unnatural prodigy, anticipating the maturity of a later age, but as a truly human child, silently lying and smiling on the bosom of his virgin mother; "growing" and "waxing strong in spirit,"[5] and therefore subject to the law of regular development, yet differing from all other children by his supernatural conception and perfect freedom from hereditary sin and guilt. He appears in the celestial beauty of unspotted innocence, a veritable flower of paradise. He was *that Holy Thing,*" according to the announcement of the angel Gabriel (Luke i. 35), admired and loved by all who approached him in a child-like spirit, but exciting the dark suspicion of the tyrant king who represented his future enemies and persecutors.

Who can measure the ennobling, purifying, and cheering influence which proceeds from the contemplation of the Christ-child, at each returning Christmas season, upon the hearts of young and old in every land and nation! The loss of the first estate is richly compensated by the undying innocence of paradise regained.

Of the BOYHOOD of Jesus we know only one fact, recorded by Luke; but it is in perfect keeping with the peculiar charm of his childhood, and foreshadows at the same time the glory of his public life as one uninterrupted service of his heavenly Father.[6] When twelve years old, we find him in the temple, in the midst of the Jewish doctors; not teaching and offending them, as in the apocryphal Gospels, by any immodesty or forwardness, but hearing and asking questions: thus actually learning from them, and yet filling them with astonishment at his understanding and answers. There is nothing premature, forced, or unbecoming his age, and yet a degree of wisdom and an intensity of interest in religion which rises far above a purely human youth. "He increased," we are told, "in wisdom and stature, and in favor with God and man" (Luke ii. 52). He was subject to his parents, and practiced all the virtues of an obedient son; and yet he filled them with a sacred awe as they saw him absorbed in "the things of his Father,"[7] and heard him utter, words which they were unable to understand at the time, but which Mary treasured up in her heart as a holy secret, convinced that they must have some deep meaning answering to the mystery of his supernatural conception and birth.

Such an idea of a harmless and faultless heavenly childhood, of a growing, learning, and yet surprisingly wise boyhood, as it meets us in living reality at the portal of the gospel history, never entered the imagination of a biographer, poet, or philosopher, before. On the contrary, as has been justly observed,[8] "in all the higher ranges of character, the excellence portrayed is never the simple unfolding of a harmonious and perfect beauty contained in the germ of childhood, but is a character formed by a process of rectification in which many follies are mended and distempers removed; in which confidence is checked by defeat, passion moderated by reason, smartness sobered by experience. Commonly a certain pleasure is taken in showing how the many wayward sallies of the boy are, at length, reduced by discipline to the character of wisdom, justice, and public heroism so much admired. Besides, if any writer, of almost any age, will undertake to: describe, not merely a spotless but a superhuman or celestial childhood, not having the reality before him, he must be somewhat more than human himself if he does not pile together a mass of clumsy exaggerations, and draw and overdraw, till neither heaven nor earth, can find any verisimilitude in the picture."

This unnatural exaggeration, into which the mythical fancy of man, in its endeavor to produce a superhuman childhood and boyhood, will inevitably fall, is strikingly exhibited in the myth of Hercules, who, while yet a suckling in the cradle, squeezed two monster serpents to death with his tender hands; and still more in the accounts of the apocryphal Gospels on the wonderful performances of the infant Saviour. These apocryphal Gospels are related to the canonical Gospels as a counterfeit to the genuine coin, or as a revolting caricature to the inimitable original; but, by the very contrast, they tend, negatively, to corroborate the truth of the evangelical history. The strange contrast has been frequently urged, especially in the Strauss-controversy, and used as an argument against the mythical theory. While the evangelists expressly reserve the performance of miracles to the age of maturity and public life, and observe a significant silence concerning the parents of Jesus, the pseudo-evangelists fill the infancy and early years of the Saviour and his mother with the strangest prodigies, and make the active intercession of Mary very prominent throughout. According to their representation, even dumb idols, irrational beasts, and senseless trees, bow in adoration before the infant Jesus on his journey to Egypt; and after his return, when yet a boy of five or seven years, he changes balls of clay into flying birds for the idle amusement of his playmates, strikes terror round about him, dries up a stream of water by a mere word, transforms his companions into goats, raises the dead to life, and performs all sorts of miraculous cures through a magical influence which proceeds from the very water in which he was washed, the towels which he used, and the bed on which he slept.[9] Here we have the falsehood and absurdity of *unnatural fiction*; while the New Testament presents to us the truth and beauty of a supernatural yet *most real history*, which shines out only in brighter colors by the contrast of the mythical shadow.

---

1. This idea is almost as old as the Christian Church, and was already pretty clearly taught by Irenæus, who, through the single link of his teacher Polycarp, stood connected with the age of St. John the apostle. He says ("*Adv. Hæreses.*" lib. ii. cap. 22, § 4): "*Omnes enim venit [Christus] per semetipsum salvare, omnes, inquam, qui per eum renascuntur in Deum, infantes et parvulos et pueros et seniores. Ideo per omnem venit ætatem et infantibus infans factus, sanctificans infantes; in parvulis parvulus, sanctificans hanc ipsam habentes ætatem, simul et exemplum illis pietatis effectus et justitiæ et subjectionis; in juvenibus juvenis, exemplum juvenibus fiens et sanctificans Domino. Sic et senior in senioribus (?), ut sit perfectus magister in omnibus,*" &c. But Irenæus erred in carrying the idea too far, and assuming Christ to have lived over fifty years, on the ground of the indefinite estimate of the Jews, John viii. 57. Hippolytus, in his recently discovered "*Philosophumena,*" expresses the same view.
2. See Luke i. 41-45: the Magnificat, or the Virgin's Song, ver. 46-55; the Benedictus, or the Song of Zacharias, ver. 67-79.
3. Bethlehem was indeed the ancestral seat of the house of David (Ruth i. 1, 2), and fortified by Rehoboam (2 Chron. xi. 16), but remained an insignificant place, and is not even mentioned among the towns of Judah in the Hebrew text of Joshua, nor in Neh. xi. 25. Comp. Mich. v. 1, where the prophet thus contrasts its insignif-

icance with its future destiny as the birthplace of the Saviour (according to the Hebrew text): "But thou Bethlehem Ephratah, too small to be among the thousands of Judah בְּאַלְפֵי יְהוּדָה—i. e., the central towns where the heads of thousands or subordinate divisions of tribes resided], out of thee shall come forth unto me One who is to be the Ruler in Israel; whose origin is from the first of time, from the days of eternity."

4. Compare the rich remarks of Dr. Lange in his commentary on the second chapter of Matthew, ver. 1-11. "*Bibelwerk*," vol. i. p. 19 ff. (Am. ed. vol. i. p. 55 ff.)

5. Luke ii. 40: τὸ παιδίον ηὔξανεν καὶ ἐκραταιοῦτο πνεύματι. "And the child grew and waxed strong in spirit;" precisely the same expression which Luke used, i. 80, of John the Baptist. Compare also, for the human growth and development of Christ, Luke ii. 52; Heb. ii. 10-18 and v. 8 and 9, where it is said that he *learned* obedience, and, being made perfect, he *became* the author of eternal salvation.

6. Dr. J. P. Lange, in his "*Leben Jesu nach den Evangelien*," Heidelberg, 1844 ff. vol. ii. p. 127, says: "The history of Jesus in his twelfth year represents his whole development. It is the characteristic deed of his youth, the revelation of his youthful life, a reflection of his birth, a sign and anticipation of his future heroic career. It represents the childhood of his ideality, therefore also the ideality of childhood in general." Compare also the suggestive remarks of Olshausen on that passage, "*Commentar*" (3d Germ. ed. vol. i. p. 145 ff.); and of Van Oosterzee, in Lange's "*Bibelwerk*."

7. Luke ii. 49: ἐν τοῖς τοῦ πατρός μου δεῖ, [δεῖ indicates a *moral* necessity which is identical with true freedom], εἶναί με. The fathers and most of the modern commentators refer the τοῖς to the house of God, or the temple. This is grammatically allowable, but restricts the sense, and deprives it of its deeper meaning; for he could only occasionally be in the temple of Jerusalem. Nearly all the English versions, Tyndale, Cranmer, the Genevan, and James, translate more correctly, "about my Father's *business*." But we object to the term *business* in this connection, and prefer the more literal translation "*in* (not *about*) *the things* (or affairs) of my Father." The *in* signifies the life-element in which Christ moved during his whole life, whether in the temple or out of it.

8. By Dr. Horace Bushnell, in his genial work, already quoted, on "*Nature and the Supernatural*," page 280 ("*The Character of Jesus*," page 19 ff.)

9. See the particulars, with ample quotations from the sources, in Rud. Hoffmaann's "*Leben Jesu nach den Apokryphen im Zusammenhang aus den Quellen erzaehlt und wissenschaftlich untersucht*." Leipzig, 1851, p. 140-263.

2

HIS TRAINING

W ITH the exception of these few but significant hints, the youth of Jesus, and the preparation for his public ministry, are enshrined in mysterious silence. But we know the outward condition and circumstances under which he grew up; and these furnish no explanation for the astounding results, without the admission of the supernatural and divine element in his life.

He grew up among a people seldom and only contemptuously named by the ancient classics, and subjected at the time to the yoke of a foreign oppressor; in a remote and conquered province of the Roman Empire; in the darkest district of Palestine; in a country-town of proverbial insignificance.[1] He spent his youth in poverty and manual labor, in the obscurity of a carpenter's shop; far away from universities, academies, libraries, and literary or polished society; without any help, as far as we know, except the parental care, the daily wonders of Nature, the Old-Testament Scriptures, the weekly Sabbath services of the synagogue at Nazareth (Luke iv. 16), the annual festivals in the Temple of Jerusalem (Luke ii. 42 ff.), and the secret intercourse of his soul with God, his heavenly Fattier. These are indeed the great educators of the mind and heart. The book of Nature and the book of Revelation are filled with richer and more important lessons than all the works of human art and learning; but they were accessible alike to every Jew, and gave no advantage to Jesus over his humblest neighbor.

Hence the question of Nathanael: "What good can come out of Nazareth?" Hence the natural surprise of the Jews, who knew all his human relations and antecedents. "How knoweth this man letters," they asked when they heard Jesus teach, "having never learned?" (John vii. 15.) And on another occasion, when he taught in the synagogue: "Whence has this man this wisdom and these mighty works? Is not this the carpenter's son? is not his mother Mary? and his brethren (brothers), James and Joses and Simon and Judas? And his sisters—are they not all with us? Whence, then, hath this man all these things?"[2] These questions are unavoidable and unanswerable, if Christ be regarded as a mere man; for each effect presupposes a corresponding cause.

The difficulty here presented can by no means be solved by a reference to the fact that many, perhaps the majority of great men, especially in the Church, have risen, by their own industry and perseverance, from the lower walks of life, and from a severe contest with poverty and obstacles of every kind. The fact itself is readily conceded; but, in every one of these cases, schools or books, or patrons and friends, or peculiar events and influences, can be pointed out as auxiliary aids in the development of intellectual or moral greatness. There is always some human or natural cause, or combination of causes, which accounts for the final result.

Luther, for instance, was indeed the son of poor peasants, and had a very hard youth: but he went to the schools of Mansfeld, Magdeburg, and Eisenach; to the university of Erfurt; passed through the ascetic discipline of convent life; studied and labored among professors, students, and libraries; and was innocently, as it were, made a reformer by extraordinary events, and the irresistible current of his age.

Shakspeare is generally and justly regarded as the most remarkable and most wonderful example of a self taught man; who, without the regular routine of school education, became the greatest dramatic poet, not only of his age and country, but of all times. But the absurd idea that the son of the Warwickshire yeoman or butcher or glover—we hardly know which—was essentially an unlearned man, and jumped with one bound from the supposed though poorly authenticated youthful folly of deer-stealing to the highest position in literature, has long since been abandoned by competent judges. It is certain that he spent several years in the free grammar-school of Stratford on Avon, where he probably acquired the "small Latin, and less Greek," which, however small in the eyes of so profound a classical scholar as Ben Jonson, was certainly large enough to make the fortune of any enterprising youth from New England. And, whatever were the defects of his training, he must have made them up by intense private study of books, and the closest observation of men and things: for his dramas—the occasional chronological, historical, and geographical mistakes notwithstanding, which are small matters at all events, and in most cases, as in "Pericles" and in "Midsummer-Night's Dream," either intentional, or mere freaks of fancy—abound in the most accurate and comprehensive knowledge of human nature under all its types and conditions,—in the cold North and the sunny South; in the fifteenth century, and at the time of Caesar, under the influence of Christianity and of Judaism,—together with a great variety of historical and other information, which can not be acquired without immense industry, and the help of oral or printed instruction. Moreover, he lived in the city of London; united the offices of actor, manager, and writer, in the classic age of Elizabeth, in the company of genial and gifted friends, with free access to the highest ranks of blood, wealth, and wit, and during the closing scenes of the greatest upheaving of the human mind which ever took place since the introduction of Christianity.[3]

In the case of Christ, no such natural explanation can be given. He can be ranked neither with the school-trained nor with the self-trained or self-made men; if by the latter we understand, as we must, those who, without the regular aid of *living* teachers, yet with the same educational *means*, such as books, the observation of men and things, and the intense application of their mental faculties, attained to vigor of intellect, and wealth of scholarship,—like Shakspeare, Jacob Boehm, Benjamin Franklin, and others. All the attempts to bring him into contact with Egyptian wisdom, or the Essenic theosophy, or other sources of learning, are without a shadow of proof, and explain nothing after all. He never quotes from books, except the Old Testament. He never refers to secular history, poetry, rhetoric, mathematics, astronomy, foreign languages, natural sciences, or any of those branches of knowledge which make up human learning and literature. He confined himself strictly to religion. But, from that center, he shed light over the whole world of man and nature. In this department, unlike all other great men, even the prophets and the apostles, he was absolutely original and independent. He taught the world as one who had learned nothing from it, and was under no obligation to it. He speaks from divine intuition, as one who not only *knows* the truth, but *is* the truth; and with an authority that commands absolute submission, or provokes rebellion, but can never be passed by with contempt or indifference. "His character and life were originated and sustained in spite of circumstances with which no earthly force could have contended, and therefore must have had their real foundation in a force which was preternatural and divine."[4]

At the same time, it is easy to see, from the admission of Christ's divinity, that by this condescension he has raised humble origin, poverty, manual labor, and the lower orders of society, to a dignity and sacredness never known before, and has revolutionized the false standard of judging the value of men and things from their outward appearance, and of associating moral worth with social elevation, and moral degradation with low rank.

---

1. Renan, in his *Life*, or *Romance* rather, of *Jesus*, chap. ii., gives a graphic description of the natural beauties of Nazareth, as among the educational influences which account for the greatness of Christ; but all this can not do away with the seclusion and proverbial insignificance of the place (John i. 48), and loses much of its force when we remember the narrow streets and filth of an Oriental town. "Nazareth," says Renan, "was a little town, situated in a fold of land broadly open at the summit of the group of mountains which closes on the north the Plain of Esdralon. The population is now from three to four thousand, and it can not have varied very much . . . . The environs are charming, and no place in the world was so well adapted to dreams of absolute happiness. Even in our days, Nazareth is a delightful sojourn,—the only place perhaps, in Palestine, where the soul feels a little relieved of the burden which weighs upon it in the midst of this unequaled desolation. The people are friendly and good-natured; the gardens are fresh and green . . . . The beauty of the women who gather there at night—this beauty which was already remarked in the sixth century, and in which was seen the gift of the

Virgin Mary (by Antonius Martyr, *Itiner.* § 5)—has been surprisingly well preserved. It is the Syrian type in all its languishing grace."

2. Matt. xiii. 54-56. Compare also Mark vi. 3: "Is not this *the carpenter, the son* of Mary?" &c.; from which it would appear that Jesus himself engaged in the trade of Joseph. This is comfirmed by ancient tradition and the custom of Jewish Rabbins. Thus St. Paul was a tent-maker (Acts xviii. 3). The profession of a carpenter was by no means degrading, but regarded among the most honorable and useful. Hence the question of the Nazarenes, "*Is not this the carpenter's son?*" is to be taken as a question of surprise rather than of contempt. They denied the social superiority, not the equality of Jesus with them; and could not understand from his social position how he could rise above the common level, and perform such wonderful works.

3. Comp. G. G. Gervinus: "*Shakspeare,*" Leipzig, 1850, vol. i. pp. 38-41. This masterly critic and expounder of the British poet pronounces him one of the best and most extensively informed men of his age: "*Es ist heute kein Wagniss mehr, zu sagen, dass Shakspeare in jener Zeit an Umfang vielfachen Wissens sehr wenige seines Gleichen gehabt habe.*"

4. John Young: "*The Christ of History,*" p. 35.

3

HIS PUBLIC LIFE

THE SHORT DURATION AND MIGHTY EFFECT OF HIS MINISTRY. ABSENCE OF ALL OSTENTATION AND WORLDLY GREATNESS.

W E now approach the public life of Jesus. In his thirtieth year, after the Messianic inauguration through the baptism by John as his immediate forerunner, and as the representative of the Old Testament, both in its legal and prophetic or evangelical aspect, and after the Messianic probation by the temptation in the wilderness,—the counterpart of the temptation of the first Adam in paradise,—he entered upon his great work.

His public life lasted only three years; and, before he had reached the age of ordinary maturity, he died, in the full beauty and vigor of early manhood, without tasting the infirmities of declining years, which would inevitably mar the picture of the Regenerator of the race, and the Prince of life. He retained the dew of his youth upon him: he never became an old man. Both his person and his work, every word he spoke, and every act he performed, has the freshness, brilliance, and vigor of youth, and will retain it to the end of time. All other things fade away; every book of man loses its interest after repeated reading: but the gospel of Jesus never wearies the reader; it becomes more interesting the more it is read, and grows deeper at every attempt to fathom its depth. Even Napoleon is reported to have said on St. Helena, pointing to a copy of the Testament on his table: "I never tire with reading it, and I read it daily with equal delight. The gospel is not a book, but a living power which overwhelms every opposing force. The soul which is captivated by the beauty of the gospel does no more belong to itself or to the world, but to God. What an evidence is this of the divinity of Christ!"

And yet, unlike all other men of his years, Christ combined, with the freshness, energy, and originating power of youth, that wisdom, moderation, and experience, which belong only to mature age. The short triennium of his public ministry contains more, even from a purely historical point of observation, than the longest life of the greatest and best of men. It is pregnant with the deepest meaning of the counsel of God and the destiny of the race. It is the ripe fruit of all preceding ages, the fulfillment of the hopes and desires of the Jewish and heathen mind, and the fruitful germ of succeeding generations,— containing the impulse to the purest thoughts and noblest actions down to the end of time. It is "the end of a boundless past, the center of a boundless present, and the beginning of a boundless future."[1]

How remarkable, how wonderful, this contrast between the short duration and the immeasurable significance of Christ's ministry! The Saviour of the world a youth!

Other men require a long succession of years to mature their mind and character, and to make a lasting impression upon the world. There are exceptions, we admit. Alexander the Great, the last and most brilliant efflorescence of the ancient Greek nationality, died a young man of thirty-three, after having conquered the East to the borders of the Indus. But who would think of comparing an ambitious warrior, conquered by his own lust, and dying a victim of his passion, with the spotless Friend of sinners? a few bloody victories of the one with the peaceful triumphs of the other? and a huge military empire of force, which crumbled to pieces as soon as it was erected, with the spiritual kingdom of truth and love which stands to this day, and will last for ever? Nor should it be forgotten, that the true significance and only value of Alexander's conquest lay beyond the horizon of his ambition and intention; and that by carrying the language and civilization of Greece to Asia, and bringing together the Oriental and Occidental world, it prepared the way for the introduction of the universal religion of Christ. Napoleon, in his conversations with Gen. Bertrand at St.

Helena, made the striking remark: "The world admires the conquest of Alexander; but Christ is a conqueror who attracts, unites to himself, and incorporates with him, for its own benefit, not a nation,—no, but the whole human race. What a miracle! The human soul, with all its faculties, becomes an annex of the existence of Christ."

There is another striking distinction of a general character, between Christ and the heroes of history, which we must notice here. We should naturally suppose that such an uncommon personage, setting up the most astounding claims and proposing the most extraordinary work, would surround himself with extraordinary circumstances, and maintain a position far above the vulgar and degraded multitude around him. We should expect something uncommon and striking in his look, his dress, his manner, his mode of speech, his outward life, and the train of his attendants.

But the very reverse is the case. His greatness is singularly unostentatious, modest, and quiet; and, far from repelling the beholder, it attracts and invites him to familiar approach. His public life never moved on the imposing arena of secular heroism, but within the humble circle of every-day life, and the simple relations of a son, a brother, a citizen, a teacher, and a friend. He had no army to command, no kingdom to rule, no prominent station to fill, no worldly favors and rewards to dispense. He was an humble individual, without friends and patrons in the Sanhedrin or at the court of Herod. He never mingled in familiar intercourse with the religious or social leaders of the nation, whom he had startled in his twelfth year by his questions and answers. He selected his disciples from among the illiterate fishermen of Galilee, and promised them no reward in this world but a part in the bitter cup of his sufferings. He dined with publicans and sinners, and mingled with the common people, without ever condescending to their low manners and habits. He was so poor, that he had no place on which to rest his head. He depended, for the supply of his modest wants, on the voluntary contributions of a few pious females; and the purse was in the hands of a thief and a traitor. Nor had he learning, art, or eloquence, in the usual sense of the term, or any other kind of power by which great men arrest the attention and secure the admiration of the world. The writers of Greece and Rome were ignorant even of his existence, until, several years after the crucifixion, the effects of his mission, in the steady growth of the sect of his followers, forced from them some contemptuous notice, and then roused them to opposition.

And yet this Jesus of Nazareth, without money and arms, conquered more millions than Alexander, Caesar, Mohammed, and Napoleon; without science and learning, he shed more light on things human and divine than all philosophers and scholars combined; without the eloquence of schools, he spoke such words of life as were never spoken before or since, and produced effects which lie beyond the reach of any orator or poet; without writing a single line, he set more pens in motion, and furnished themes for more sermons, orations, discussions, learned volumes, works of art, and sweet songs of praise, than the whole army of great men of ancient and modern times. Born in a manger, and crucified as a malefactor, he now controls the destinies of the civilized world, and rules a spiritual empire which embraces one-third of the inhabitants of the globe. There never was in this world a life so unpretending, modest, and lowly in its outward form and condition. and yet producing such extraordinary effects upon all ages, nations, and classes of men. The annals of history produce no other example of such complete and astounding success, in spite of the absence of those material, social, literary, and artistic powers and influences which are indispensable to success for a mere man. Christ stands, in this respect also, solitary and alone among all the heroes of history, and presents to us an insolvable problem, unless we admit him to be more than man, even the eternal Son of God.

We will now attempt to describe his personal or moral and religious character as it appears in the record of his public life, and then examine his own testimony of himself as giving us the only rational solution of this mighty problem.

---

1. Heinrich Steffens, a follower of Schelling, and a Christian philosopher, speaks thus of man, and bases upon this thought his "System of Anthropology." But it may be applied in its fullest and absolute sense to Christ, as the ideal man, in whom and through whom alone the race can become complete.

4

HIS FREEDOM FROM SIN

THE first impression which we receive from the life of Jesus is that of perfect innocency and sinlessness in the midst of a sinful world. He, and he alone, carried the spotless purity of childhood untarnished through his youth and manhood. Hence the lamb and the dove are his appropriate symbols.

He was, indeed, tempted as we are; but he never yielded to temptation.[1] His sinlessness was at first only the *relative* sinlessness of Adam before the fall; which implies the necessity of trial and temptation, and the peccability, or the possibility of the fall. Had he been endowed with absolute impeccability from the start, he could not be a true man, nor our model for imitation: his holiness, instead of being his own self-acquired act and inherent merit, would be an accidental or outward gift, and his temptation an unreal show. As a true man, Christ must have been a free and responsible moral agent: freedom implies the power of choice between good and evil, and the power of disobedience as well as obedience to the law of God. But here is the great fundamental difference between the first and the second Adam: the first Adam lost his innocence by the abuse of his freedom, and fell, by his own act of disobedience, into the dire necessity of sin; while the second Adam was innocent in the midst of sinners, and maintained his innocence against all and every temptation. Christ's *relative* sinlessness became more and more *absolute* sinlessness by his own moral act, or the right use of his freedom in perfect active and passive obedience to God. In other words, Christ's original *possibility of not sirning*,[2] which includes the opposite possibility of sinning, but excludes the actuality of sin, was unfolded into the *impossibility of sinning*,[3] which can not sin because it *will* not. This is the highest stage of freedom where it becomes identical with moral necessity, or absolute and unchangeable self-determination for goodness and holiness. This is the freedom of God, and also of the saints in heaven; with this difference,—that the saints obtain that position by deliverance and salvation from sin and death, while Christ acquired it by his own merit[4].

In vain we look through the entire biography of Jesus for a single stain or the slightest shadow on his moral character. There never lived a more harmless being on earth. He injured nobody, he took advantage of nobody. He never spoke an improper word, he never committed a wrong action. He exhibited a uniform elevation above the objects, opinions, pleasures, and passions of this world, and disregard to riches, displays, fame, and favor of men. "No vice that has a name can be thought of in connection with Jesus Christ.

Ingenious malignity looks in vain for the faintest trace of self-seeking in his motives; sensuality shrinks abashed from his celestial purity; falsehood can leave no stain on Him who is incarnate truth; injustice is forgotten beside his errorless equity; the very possibility of avarice is swallowed up in his benignity and love; the very idea of ambition is lost in his divine wisdom and divine self abnegation."[5]

The apparent outbreak of passion in the expulsion of the profane traffickers from the temple is the only instance on the record of his history which might be quoted against his freedom from the faults of humanity. But the very effect which it produced shows that, far from being the outburst of passion, the expulsion was a judicial act of a religious reformer, vindicating, in just and holy zeal, the honor of the Lord of the temple. It was an exhibition, not of weakness, but of dignity and majesty, which at once silenced the offenders, though superior in number and physical strength, and made them submit to their well-deserved punishment without a murmur, and in awe of the presence of a superhuman power. The cursing of the unfruitful fig-tree can still less be urged; as it evidently was a significant symbolical act, foreshadowing the fearful doom of the impenitent Jews in the destruction of Jerusalem. On the contrary, these two facts become fully intelligible only by the assumption of the presence of the Divinity in Christ; for they represent him as the Lord of the temple, and as the Lord of creation.

The perfect innocence of Jesus, however, is based, not only negatively on the absence of any recorded word or act to the contrary, and his absolute exemption from every trace of selfishness and worldliness, but positively also, on the unanimous testimony of John the Baptist, and the apostles who bowed before the majesty of his character in unbounded veneration, and declare him "just," "holy," and "without sin."[6] It is admitted, moreover, by his enemies,—the heathen judge Pilate, and his wife, representing, as it were, the Roman law and justice when they shuddered with fear, and Pilate washed his hands to be clear of innocent blood; by the rude Roman centurion confessing under the cross, in the name of the disinterested spectators: "Truly this was the Son of God;" and by Judas himself, the immediate witness of his whole public and private life, exclaiming in despair: "I sinned in betraying innocent blood."[7] Even dumb nature responded in mysterious sympathy; and the beclouded heavens above, and the shaking earth beneath, united in paying their unconscious tribute to the divine purity of their dying Lord.

The objection that the evangelists were either not fully informed concerning the facts, or mistaken in their estimate of the character of Christ, is of no avail. For, in addition to their testimony, we have his own personal conviction of entire freedom from sin and unworthiness; which leaves us only the choice between absolute moral purity and absolute hypocrisy: such hypocrisy would indeed be both the greatest miracle and the greatest moral monstrosity on record.

The very fact that Christ came for the express purpose of saving sinners, implies his own consciousness of personal freedom from guilt and from all need of salvation. And this is the unmistakable impression made upon us by his whole public life and conduct. He nowhere shows the least concern for his own salvation, but knows himself to be in undisturbed harmony with his heavenly Father. While calling most

earnestly upon all others to repent, he stood in no need of conversion
and regeneration, but simply of the regular harmonious unfolding of
his moral powers. While directing all his followers, in the fourth peti-
tion of his model prayer, to ask daily for the forgiveness of their sins as
well as their daily bread, he himself never asked God for pardon and
forgiveness except in behalf of others. While freely conversing with
sinners, he always did so with the love and interest of a Saviour of
sinners. He always did so: this is the historical fact, no matter how you
may explain it. And, to remove every doubt, we have his open and
fearless challenge to his bitter enemies: "Which of you convinceth me
of sin?"[8] In this question, which remains unanswered to this day, he
clearly exempts himself from the common fault and guilt of the race. In
the mouth of any other man, this question would at once betray either
the hight of hypocrisy, or a degree of self-deception bordering on
madness itself, and would overthrow the very foundation of all human
goodness; while, from the mouth of Jesus, we instinctively receive it as
the triumphant self-vindication of one who stood far above the possibility of successful impeachment or founded suspicion.

The assumption that Christ was a sinner, and knew himself such,
although he professed the contrary, and made upon friends and enemies
the impression of spotless innocency, is the most monstrous deception
that can well be imagined. "If Jesus was a sinner, he was conscious of
sin as all sinners are, and therefore was a hypocrite in the whole fabric
of his character; realizing, so much of divine beauty in it, maintaining
the show of such unfaltering harmony and celestial grace, and doing all
this with a mind confused and fouled by the affectations acted for true
virtues! Such an example of successful hypocrisy would be itself the
greatest miracle ever heard of in the world."[9]

It is an indisputable fact, then, both from his mission and uniform
conduct, and his express declaration, that Christ *knew* himself free
from sin and guilt. The only rational explanation of this fact is that
Christ was no sinner. And this is readily conceded by the greatest
divines, even those who are by no means regarded as orthodox.[10] The
admission of this fact implies the further admission, that Christ differed
from all other men, not in degree only, but in *kind*. For although we
must utterly repudiate the pantheistic notion of the necessity of sin, and

maintain that human nature in itself considered is capable of sinless-ness, that it was sinless, in fact, before the fall, and that it will ulti-mately become sinless again by the redemption of Christ,—yet it is equally certain that human nature in its *present* condition is not sinless, and never has been since the fall, except in the single case of Christ; and that, for this very reason, Christ's sinlessness can only be explained on the ground of such an extraordinary indwelling of God in him as never took place in any other human being before or after.

The Bible, the conscience of man, and the daily experience of life, unite in testifying to the universal fact of sin, no matter how we may explain it. Sin is the deep, dark mystery of existence, the stumbling-block to reason, the problem of problems, the fruitful source of all misery and woe. The literature of all nations and ages is full of lamen-tations over this most awful and most stubborn of all facts. Even heathen philosophers, historians, and poets acknowledge it in the strongest terms. "The evil passions," says Plutarch, "are inborn in man, and were not introduced from without; and, if strict discipline would not come to aid, man would hardly be tamer than the wildest beast." The well-known line of the Roman poet:—

"Video meliora proboque, deteriora sequor;"

and that other:—

"Nitimur in vetitum semper cupimusque negata,"—

have often been quoted as a striking response of the heathen conscience and experience to the inspired description of this ethical conflict betwen heaven and hell in every soul (Rom. vii.). And as to the actual condition of morals in the age of Christ and the apostles, Seneca, Tacitus, Persius, and Juvenal give the most unfavorable accounts, which fully corroborate the dark picture of St. Paul in the first chapter of his Epistle to the Romans.

"All is full of crime and vice," says Seneca: "they are open and manifest: iniquity prevails in every heart, and innocence has not only become rare, but has entirely disappeared." Marcus Aurelius, the Stoic philosopher on the throne and the persecutor of Christians, complains that "faithfulness, the sense of honor, righteousness and truth, have taken their flight from the wide earth to heaven."

If this is the testimony of the sages of heathenism, what shall we say of the Christian, whose sense of sin and guilt is deepened and sharpened in proportion to his knowledge of God's holiness and his experience of God's redeeming grace. The entire Christian world, Greek, Latin, and Protestant, agree in the scriptural doctrine of the universal depravity of human nature since the apostasy of the first Adam. Even the modern and unscriptural dogma of the Roman Catholic Church, that the Virgin Mary was free from hereditary as well as actual sin, can hardly be quoted as an exception; for her sinlessness is explained, in the papal decision of 1854, by the assumption of a miraculous interposition of divine favor, and the reflex influence of the merits of her Son. There is not a single mortal who has not to charge himself with some defect or folly; and man's consciousness of sin and unworthiness deepens just in proportion to his self-knowledge, and progress in virtue and goodness. There is not a single saint who has not experienced a new birth from above, and an actual conversion from sin to holiness, and who does not feel daily the need of repentance and divine forgiveness. The very greatest and best of them, as St. Paul and St. Augustine, passed through a violent struggle and a radical revolution; and their whole theological system and religious experience rest on the felt antithesis of sin and grace.

But in Christ we have the one solitary and absolute exception to this universal rule,—an individual thinking like a man, feeling like a man, speaking, acting, suffering, and dying like a man, surrounded by sinners in every direction, with the keenest sense of sin, and the deepest sympathy with sinners, commencing his public ministry with the call: "Repent; for the kingdom of heaven is at hand" (Matt. iv. 17); yet never touched in the least by the contamination of the world; never putting himself in the attitude of a sinner before God; never shedding a tear of repentance; never regretting a single thought, word, or deed; never needing or asking divine pardon; never concerned about the salvation of his own soul; and boldly facing all his present and future enemies, in the absolute certainty of his spotless purity before God and man.

---

1. Comp. with the history of the temptation in the wilderness, Matt. iv. and Luke iv., the significant passages in the Epistle to the Hebrews, iv. 15, "Tempted in all points as we are, yet without sin" (πεπειρασμένον κατὰ πάντα καθ' ὁμοιότητα χωρὶς ἁμαρτίας), and v. 8 "Though he was a son, yet learned he obedience by the things which he suffered" (καίπερ ὢν υἱός, ἔμαθεν ἀφ' ὧν ἔπαθεν τὴν ὑπακοήν, καὶ τελειωθεὶς ἐγένετο, κ. τ. λ.)
2. In scholastic terminology, the *posse non peccare*, or the *impeccabilitas minor*. To this corresponds the *posse non mori*, or the *immortalitas minor*, i. e. the relative or conditional immortality of Adam in Paradise, which depended on his probation, and was lost by the fall.
3. The *non posse peccare*, or the *impeccabilitas major*. With this is closely connected the *non posse mori*, or the *immortalitas major*, the absolute immortality of the resurrection-state, which can never be lost.
4. The Rev. Dr. Jos. Berg, professor in the Theological Seminary at New Brunswick, in a friendly notice of the first edition of this essay (in his "Evangelical Quarterly" for April, 1861, p. 289), objects to this view of the peccability of the man Jesus, as being inconsistent with his absolute holiness. But I can not see the force of his objection. Peccability is merely the *possibility* of sin, such as attached also to Adam in the state of innocence; and it by no means involves Christ in the reality of sin, either original or actual. Against such an inference the language of the text is sufficiently guarded. It is true, the angel called Christ the *Holy Thing* from the moment of his conception, τὸ γεννώμενον ἅγιον (Luke i. 35). But was not Adam holy too, though "subject to fall"? (as the *Larger Westminster Confession* expresses it, qu. 17.) Moreover, this original holiness can not exclude the idea of the development and physical and moral growth of the Christ-child; for this is distinctly asserted by the same evangelist, Luke ii. 40, 52: comp. Heb. v. 8. The denial of the *possibility* of sin overthrows the realness of Christ's humanity, and turns the history of the temptation into a Gnostic phantom and mere sham. It is just because Christ was really and actually tempted, and this not only by the Devil in the wilderness (Matt. iv.), but throughout his whole life (Luke xxii. 28, Heb. iv. 15), and because he successfully resisted the temptation under every form, that he became both our Saviour and our Example: comp. Heb. v. 7-9.
5. Peter Bayne: "*The Testimony of Christ to Christianity.*" Boston, 1862, pp. 105.
6. Comp. Acts iii. 14; 1 Pet. i. 19; ii. 22; iii. 18; 2 Cor. v. 21; 1 John ii. 29; iii. 5, 7; Heb. iv. 15; vii. 26. Considering the infinite superiority of the ethics of the apostles to the ethics of the ancient Greeks, it is absurd to weaken the force of this unanimous testimony (as is done by D. F. Strauss, "*Die christliche Glaubenslehre,*" vol. ii. p. 192; and to some extent even by Hase, "*Leben Jesu,*" p. 61) by a reference to Xenophon's estimate of Socrates: "No one ever saw Socrates do, or heard him say, any thing impious or unholy" (Οὐδεὶς πώποτε Σωκράτους οὐδὲν ἀσεβὲς οὐδὲ ἀνόσιον οὔτε π᾽ άττοντος εἶδεν, οὔτε λέγοντος ἤκουσεν.

—Memorab., i. 11). In the best case, this is only a negative judgment of his conduct, and not of the state of his heart; and acquits Socrates of all manifestation of impiety, without attributing to him, positively, religious or moral perfection. Moreover, it is a very different thing to assert of a man that he was free from sin and error, and to set forth in actual life a consistent sinless character. The purest man, if he were to invent such a character, would inevitably mix up with it some traits of human imperfection, or overdraw the picture beyond the truly human sphere. But the gospel-picture of Christ strikes us throughout as perfectly original and truthful, and maintains its spotless purity in every trait, and under every situation and temptation.

7. Matt. xxvii. 19, 24-54; Luke xxiii. 22-47; Matt. xxvii. 4.

8. John viii. 46. Compare the commentators and the reflections of Ullmann, 1. c. p. 92 ff.

9. Quoted from Dr. H. Bushnell, 1. c. p. 325. The sinlessness of Jesus is denied by D. F. Strauss, in his two destructive works, *"The Life of Jesus,"* and *"The Dogmatics in Conflict with Modern Science;"* and this mainly from the *à-priori* philosophical argument of the impossibility of sinlessness, or the pantheistic notion of the inseparableness of sin from all finite existence. The only exegetical proof he urges (*"Dogmat.,"* ii. 192) is Christ's word, Matt. xix. 17: "There is none good but one, that is God." But Christ answers here to the preceding question, and the implied misconception of goodness. He does not decline the epithet *good* as such, but only in the superficial sense of the rich youth who regarded him simply as a distinguished Rabbi and a *good* man, not as one with God. He did not say, *I am not good*; but, None is good, no man is good,—much less in comparison with God. In other words, he rejected not so much the title *Good Master*, as that spirit and state of mind which looked upon him only as an exemplar of worldly wisdom and morality. In no case can he be supposed to have contradicted his own testimony concerning his innocence. See the commentators *ad locum*, especially Olshausen, Meyer, and Lange. A French writer, F. Pecaut, *"Le Christ et la Conscience,"* Paris, 1859, likewise denies the sinlessness of Christ. Pecaut refers to the following facts as evidences of moral imperfection,—the conduct of Jesus toward his mother in his twelfth year, his rebuke administered to her at the wedding feast of Cana, his expulsion of the profane traffickers from the temple, his cursing of the unfruitful fig-tree, the destruction of the herd of swine, his bitter invectives against the Pharisees, and his own rejection of the attribute *good* in the dialogue with the rich youth. But all these difficulties are of easy solution, and not to be compared with the difficulties on the other side as presented in the text. On the other hand, Pecaut himself, inconsistently enough, admits in a very eloquent passage that Christ's moral character rose beyond comparison above that of any other great man in antiquity, and was wholly penetrated by God. How, in the name of logic, is it possible to admit so much of goodness, and yet to impeach his veracity when he claims to be entirely free from sin, and equal with God? Veracity and honesty are the very foundation of a good character, and there can be no morality without them. Compare also, against Pecaut, the remarks of Dr. Van Oozterzee in his work on Christ, German translation, page 166 ff.

10. So Schleiermacher, the greatest theological genius since Calvin, in his work, *"Der christliche Glaube,"* 3d edition (1836), vol. ii. p. 78: *"Christus war von allen*

andern Menschen unterschieden durch seine wesentliche Unsündlichkeit und seine schlechthinige Vollkommenheit;" i.e., "Christ differed from all other men by his essential sinlessness and his absolute perfection;" a proposition which Schleiermacher most ably establishes not only in his "*Dogmatics,*" but also in many of his sermons. Karl Hase, "*Leben Jesu,*" 4th edition, 1854, page 60 (Clarke's English translation, Boston, 1860, p. 54), likewise admits that Christ was free from sin.

5

HIS PERFECT HOLINESS

A SINLESS Saviour, surrounded by a sinful world, is an astounding fact indeed; a sublime moral miracle in history. But this freedom from the common sin and guilt of the race is, after all, only the negative side of his character; which rises in magnitude as we contemplate the positive side,—namely, absolute moral and religious perfection.

It is universally admitted, even by deists and rationalists, that Christ taught the purest and sublimest system of ethics, one which throws all the moral precepts and maxims of the wisest men of antiquity far into the shade. The Sermon on the Mount alone is worth infinitely more than all that Confucius, Cakya-Mouni, Zoroaster, Socrates, and Seneca ever said or wrote on duty and virtue. Men of the world can hardly resist its power. Napoleon Bonaparte had it once read to him and his friends in the solitude of exile by a son of Count De Las Cases, and "expressed himself struck with the highest admiration of the purity, the sublimity, the beauty of the morality which it contained." De Las Cases, who relates this fact in his Memoires, adds: "We all experienced the same feeling."

But the difference between Christ and the great moralists of ancient or modern times is still greater if we come to the more difficult task of practice. All the systems of moral philosophy combined could not

43

regenerate the world. Words are nothing unless they are supported by deeds. A holy life is a far greater power for good than the finest moral maxim or essay. In this respect, the difference between Jesus and the great sages is so radical and fundamental, that all comparison ceases. Cicero, who, with all his excessive vanity, was one of the noblest and purest of old Roman characters, confessed that he never found a perfect sage in his life, and that philosophy only taught how he ought to be if he should ever appear on earth. It is well known that the wisest men of Greece and Rome sanctioned slavery, oppression, revenge, infanticide or exposure of infants, polygamy or concubinage, and worse vices; or, like the avaricious and venal Seneca, belied even their purer moral maxims by their conduct.[1] The greatest saints of the Old Testament, even with the help of divine grace, did not rise above reproach; and some of them are stained with the guilt of blood and adultery. It may be safely asserted, that the wisest and best of men, even among Christian nations, never live up to their own imperfect standard of excellency.

But how is it with Christ? He fully carried out his perfect doctrine in his life and conduct. He both *was* and *did* that which he *taught*: he preached his own life, and lived his own doctrine. He is the living incarnation of the ideal standard of virtue and holiness, and universally acknowledged to be the highest model for all that is pure and good and noble in the sight of God and man. Even unbelievers must admit this fact. "Christ unites in himself," says the late Theodore Parker, "the sublimest precepts and divinest practices, thus more than realizing the dream of prophets and sages; rises free from all prejudice of his age, nation, or sect; gives free range to the Spirit of God in his breast; sets aside the law, sacred and true, honored as it was,—its forms, its sacrifice, its temple, its priests; puts away the doctors of the laws—subtle, irrefragable; and pours out a doctrine beautiful as the light, sublime as heaven, and true as God."[2] And Renan, much as he perverts the life and character of Jesus, freely acknowledges, that both in word and in work, in the doctrine and practice of morality, the hero of Nazareth "is without an equal;" that "his glory remains perfect, and will be renewed for ever."[3]

We find Christ moving in all ordinary and essential relations of life,[4] as a son, a brother, a friend, a citizen, a teacher, at home and in public. We find him among all classes of society,—with sinners and saints; with the poor and the wealthy; with the sick and the healthy; with little children, grown men and women; with plain fishermen and learned scribes; with despised publicans and honored members of the Sanhedrin; with friends and foes; with admiring disciples and bitter persecutors; now with an individual, as Nicodemus or the woman of Samaria; now in the familiar circle of the twelve; now in the crowds of the people. We find him in all situations,—in the synagogue and the temple; at home and on journeys; in villages and the city of Jerusalem; in the desert and on the mountain; along the banks of Jordan and the shores of the Galilean Sea; at the joyous wedding-feast and the solemn grave; in the awful agony of Gethsemane; in the judgment-hall, before the high-priest, the king, the Roman governor, rude soldiers, and the fanatical multitude; and at last in the bitter pains of the cross on Calvary.

In all these various relations, conditions, and situations, as they are crowded within the few years of his public ministry, he sustains the same consistent character throughout, without ever exposing himself to censure. As God, according to the Bible, is one and the same always, so also Christ, according to the gospel. Guizot (in his recently published "Meditations on the Essence of the Christian Religion") justly remarks: "The most perfect, the most constant unity reigns in Jesus, in his life as in his soul, in his words as in his acts. He progresses according to the circumstances in which he lives; but his progress produces in him no change of character or design. As he appeared already in his twelfth year in the temple, full of the sense of his divine nature, so he remains and manifests himself during the whole course of his public mission. . . . . Everywhere, and under all circumstances, he is animated by the same spirit, he sheds the same light, he proclaims the same law." He fulfills every duty to God, to man, and to himself, with perfect ease and freedom, and exhibits an entire conformity to the law, in the spirit as well as the letter. His life is one unbroken service of God in active and passive obedience to his holy will; one grand act of absolute love to God and love to man; of personal self-consecration to the glory of his heavenly Father, and the salvation of a fallen race. In the language of the people who were "beyond measure astonished at his works," we must say, the more we study his life: "He did all things well."[5] In a solemn appeal to his heavenly Father in the parting hour, he could proclaim to the world that he had glorified him in the earth, and finished the work he gave him to do (John xvii. 3, 22).

---

1. Cicero, *Quæst. Tuscul.*, ii. 22: "*Quem* [*in quo erit perfecta sapientia*] *adhuc nos quidem vidimus neninem, sed philosophorum sententiis, qualis futurus sit, si modo aliquando fuerit, exponitur.*" The same writer, in the same work, ii. 4, speaks in the strongest terms of the gross contrast between the doctrine and the life of the philosophers; and Quintilian accuses them of concealing the worst vices under the name of the ancient philosophy (*Instit.* i. *Prœm.*). The virtue of chastity, in our Christian sense, was almost unknown among the heathen. Woman was essentially a slave of man's lower passions. It is notorious that disreputable women, called ἑταῖραι, or *amicæ*, were attached in Corinth to the Temple of Aphrodite, ant) enjoyed the sanction of religion for the practice of vice These dissolute characters were esteemed above housewives, and became the proper representatives of fe male culture and social elegance. Remember Aspasia Phryne, Laïs, Theodora, who attracted the admiration and courtship even of earnest philosophers like Socrates, and statesmen like Pericles. To the question of Socrates, "Is there any one with whom you converse less than with the wife?" his pupil Aristobulus replied, "No one, or at least very few." Worse than this, the disgusting vice of pæderastia, which even depraved nature abhors, was practiced as a national habit among the Greeks, without punishment or dishonor; was freely dis cussed, commended, and(praised by their poets and philosophers, and likewise divinely sanctioned by the lewdness of Jupiter with Ganymede. Dr. Döllinger, in his very instructive and learned work, "*Heidenthum und Judenthum*," 1857, p. 684 ff., sums up his investigation on this subject with the following statement: "*Bei den Griechen tritt das Laster der Pœderastie mit allen Symptomen einer grossen nationalen Krankheit, gleichsam eines ethischen Miasma auf; es zeigt sich als ein Gefühl, das stärker und heftiger wirkte, als die Weiberliebe bei anderen Volkern, massloser, leidenschaftlicher in seinen Ansbrüchen war. Rasende Eifersucht, unbedingte Hingebung, sinnliche Gluth, zärtliche Tändelei, nächtliches Weilen vor der Thüre des Geliebten, Alles, was zur Carricatur der natürlichen Geschlechtsliebe gehört, findet sich dabei. Auch die ernstesten Moralisten waren in der Beurtheilung des Verhältnisses höchst nachsichtig, sie behandelten die Sache häufig mehr mit leichtsinnigem Scherze, und duldeten die Schuldigen in ihrer Gesellschaft. In der gauzen Literatur der vorchristlichen Periode ist kaum ein Schriftsteller zu finden, der sich entschieden dagegen erklärt hatte. Vielmehr war die ganze Gesellschaft davon angesteckt, und man athmete das Miasma, so zu sagen, mit der Luft ein.*" On the whole subject of heathen morals, compare this work of Döllinger; also C. Schmidt, "*Essai historique sur la société dans le*

monde romain, et sur la transformation par le Christianisme, Paris, 1853; and Schaff, "*History of the Apostolic Church*," p. 147 ff., 157 ff., 443 ff., 454 ff.; and "*History of the Christian Church, from Christ to Constantine*," p. 302 ff.

2. Theodore Parker: "Discourses of Religion," p. 294.

3. Renan makes some striking admissions on this point, though not unmixed with error. "Morality," he says in the fifth chapter of his "*Vie de Jésus*," "is not composed of principles more or less well expressed. The poetry of the precept which makes it lovely is more than the precept itself, taken as an abstract verity. Now, it can not be denied that the maxims borrowed by Jesus from his predecessors" [Christ borrowed nothing from anybody] "produce in the gospel an effect totally different from that in the ancient Law, in the *Pirke Aboth*, or in the *Talmud*. It is not the ancient Law, it is not the Talmud, which has conquered and changed the world. Little original in itself [?], if by that is meant that it can be recomposed almost entirely with more ancient maxims, the evangelical morality remains none the less the highest creation which has emanated from the human consciousness, the most beautiful code of perfect life that any moralist has traced (*la morale évangélique n'en reste pas moins la plus haute création qui soit sortie de la conscience humaine, le plus beau code de la vie parfaite qu'aucun moraliste ait tracé*)." . . . "Jesus, son of Sirach, and Hillel, had enunciated aphorisms almost as lofty as those of Jesus. Hillel, however, will never be considered the real founder of Christianity. In morality, as in art, words are nothing; deeds are every thing. The idea which is concealed beneath a picture of Raphael is a small thing: it is the picture alone that counts. Likewise, in morality, truth becomes of value only if it pass to the condition of feeling; and it attains all its preciousness only when it is realized in the world as a fact. Men of indifferent morals have written very good maxims. Men very virtuous, also, have done nothing to continue the tradition of their virtue in the world. The palm belongs to him who has been mighty in word and in work; who has felt the truth, and, at the price of his blood, has made it triumph. Jesus, from this double point of view, is without equal: his glory remains complete, and will be renewed for ever. (*Jésus, à ce double point de vue, est sans égal; sa gloire reste entière et sera toujours renouvelée.*)"

4. The relation of husband and father must be excepted, on account of his elevation above all equal partnership, and the universalness of his character and mission, which requires the entire community of the redeemed as his bride instead of any individual daughter of Eve.

5. Mark vii. 37. The expression of the people, καλῶσ πάντα πεποίηκε (*bene omnia fecit*), must be taken as a general judgment, inferred not only from the particular case related before, but from all they had heard and seen of Christ.

6

UNITY OF VIRTUE AND PIETY

THE first feature in this singular perfection of Christ's character which strikes our attention is the perfect harmony of virtue and piety, of morality and religion, or of love to God and love to man. He is more than moral, and more than pious: he is holy in the strict and full sense of the word. There is a divine beauty and perfection in his character, the mere contemplation of which brings purity, brightness, peace, and bliss to the soul.

Piety was the soul of his morality, and lifted it far above the sphere of legality or conformity to law. Every moral action in him proceeded from supreme love to God, and looked to the temporal and eternal welfare of man. The groundwork of his character was the most intimate and uninterrupted union and communion with his heavenly Father, from whom he derived, to whom he referred, every thing. Already in his twelfth year he found his life-element end delight in the things of his Father (Luke ii. 49). It was his daily food to do the will of Him that sent him, and to finish his work (John iv. 34; comp. v. 30). To him he looked in prayer before every important act, and taught his disciples that model prayer, which, for simplicity, brevity, comprehensiveness, and suitableness, can never be surpassed. He often retired to a mountain or solitary place for prayer, and spent days and nights in this blessed privilege. But so constant and uniform was his habit of communion with the great Jehovah, that he kept it up amid the multitude, and converted the crowded city into a religious retreat. His self-consciousness was at every moment conditioned, animated, and impregnated by the consciousness of God. Even when he exclaimed in indescribable anguish of body and soul, and in vicarious sympathy with the misery of the whole race: "My God, my God, why hast thou forsaken me?"[1] the bond of union was not broken, or even loosened, but simply obscured for a moment, as the sun by a passing cloud; and the enjoyment, not the possession, of it was for a moment withdrawn from his feelings: for immediately afterward he triumphantly exclaimed: "It is finished!" and commended his soul into the hands of his Father. So strong and complete was this moral union of Christ with God at every moment of his life, that he fully realized the idea of religion whose object is to bring about such a union, and that he is the personal representative and living embodiment of Christianity as the true and absolute religion.

With all this, the piety of Christ was no inactive contemplation, or retiring mysticism, and selfish enjoyment, but thoroughly practical, ever active in works of charity, and tending to regenerate and transform the world into the kingdom of God. "He went about doing good." His life is an unbroken series of good works and virtues in active exercise; all proceeding from the same union with God, animated by the same love, and tending to the same end,—the glory of God, and the happiness of man.

---

1. Matt. xxvii. 46. It should be remembered that Jesus speaks here in the prophetical and typical words of David, Ps. xxii. 2; while, when speaking in his own language, he uniformly addresses God as his Father. Compare also the instructive reflections of Dr. Lange, in his commentary on this passage, Am. edition, pp. 526, 530.

7

COMPLETENESS AND UNIVERSALITY
OF HIS CHARACTER

THE next feature we would notice is the completeness or pleromatic fullness of the moral and religious character of Christ. While all other men represent, at best, but broken fragments of the idea of goodness and holiness, he exhausts the list of virtues and graces which may be named. His soul is a moral paradise full of charming flowers, shining in every variety of color under the blue dome of the skies, drinking in the refreshing dews of heaven and the warming beams of the sun, sending its sweet fragrance around, and filling the beholder with rapturous delight.

History exhibits to us many men of commanding and comprehensive genius, who stand at the head of their age and nation, and furnish material for the intellectual activity of whole generations and periods, until they are succeeded by other heroes at a new epoch of development. As rivers generally spring from high mountains, so knowledge and moral power rise and are ever nourished from the hights of humanity.

Abraham, the father of the faithful; Moses, the lawgiver of the Jewish theocracy; Elijah among the prophets; Peter, Paul, and John among the apostles; Athanasius and Chrysostom among the Greek, Augustine and Jerome among the Latin, fathers; Anselm and Thomas Aquinas among the schoolmen; Leo I. and Gregory VII. among the popes; Luther and Calvin in the line of Protestant reformers and divines; Socrates, the patriarch of the ancient schools of philosophy; Homer, Dante, Shakspeare and Milton, Goethe and Schiller, in the history of poetry among the various nations to which they belong; Raphael among painters; Charlemagne, the first and greatest in the long succession of German emperors; Napoleon, towering high above all the generals of his training; Washington, the wisest and best, as well as the first, of American presidents, and the purest and noblest type of the American character,—may be mentioned as examples of those representative heroes in history who anticipate and concentrate the powers of whole generations.

But all these characters represent only sectional, never universal, humanity: they are identified with a particular people or age, and partake of their errors, superstitions, and failings, almost in the same proportion in which they exhibit their virtues. Moses, though revered by the followers of three religions, was a Jew in views, feelings, habits, and position, as well as by parentage; Socrates never rose above the Greek type of character; Luther was a German in all his virtues and faults, in his strength and weakness, and can only be properly understood as a German; Calvin, though an exile from his native land, remained a Frenchman; and Washington can be to no nation on earth what he is to the American. The influence of these great men may and does extend far beyond their respective national horizons; yet they can never furnish a universal model for imitation. We regard them as extraordinary but fallible and imperfect men, whom it would be very unsafe to follow in every view and line of conduct. Very frequently, the failings and vices of great men are in proportion to their virtues and powers, as the tallest bodies cast the longest shadows. Even the three leading apostles are models of piety and virtue only as far as they reflect the image of their heavenly Master; and it is with this express limitation that Paul exhorts his spiritual children: "Be ye followers of me, even as I also am of Christ."[1]

What these representative men were to particular ages or nations or sects, or particular schools of science and art, Christ was to the human family at large in its relation to God. He, and he alone, is the universal type for universal imitation. Hence he could, without the least impropriety, or suspicion of vanity, call upon all men to forsake all things, and to follow him.[2] He stands above the limitations of age, school, sect, nation, and race. He was indeed an Israelite as to the flesh; walked about in the dress of a Jewish rabbi, and not of a Greek philosopher; and conformed, no doubt, to the Jewish habits of daily life. But this was his merest outside. If we look at his inner man, his thoughts and actions, they are of universal significance. There is nothing Jewish about him that is not at the same time found among other nations. The particular and national in him is always duly subordinated to the general and human. Still less was he ever identified with a party or sect. He was equally removed from the stiff formalism of the Pharisees, the loose liberalism of the Sadducees, and the inactive mysticism of the Essenes. He rose above all the prejudices, bigotries, and superstitions of his age and people, which exert their power even upon the strongest and otherwise most liberal minds.

Witness his freedom in the observance of the Sabbath, by which he offended the scrupulous literalists, while he fulfilled, as the Lord of the Sabbath, the true spirit of the law in its universal and abiding significance;[3] his reply to the disciples, when they traced the misfortune of the blind man to a particular sin of the subject or his parents;[4] his liberal conduct toward the Samaritans, as contrasted with the inveterate hatred and prejudice of the Jews, including his own disciples, at the time;[5] and his charitable judgment of the slaughtered Galileans whose blood Pilate had mingled with their sacrifices, and the eighteen upon whom the tower in Siloam fell and slew them (Luke xiii. 1-4). "Think ye," he addressed the children of superstition, "that these men were sinners above all the Galileans, and above all men that dwelt in Jerusalem, because they suffered such things? I tell you, Nay; but, except ye repent, ye shall all likewise perish." The only instance of Christ's complicity with popular error and superstition, which rationalists can point to with some degree of plausibility, is his belief in the devil and in demons. But they may say what they please against such a belief as irrational; experience everywhere disproves their arguments: while they get rid of *one* devil, they cannot deny the *many* devils in human shape, and leave them even more inexplicable; for it is much more irrational to believe in the continued existence of a chaotic wilderness of bad men and principles, than in an organized empire of evil with a controlling head.

As the pyramid rises high above the plains of Egypt, so Christ towers above all human teachers and founders of sects and religions. lie is, in the language of Renan, "a man of colossal" (we may well add, of infinite) "dimensions." He found disciples and worshipers among the Jews, although he identified himself with none of their sects and traditions; among the Greeks, although he proclaimed no new system of philosophy; among the Romans, although he fought no battle, and founded no worldly empire; among the Hindoos, who despise all men of low caste; among the black savages of Africa, the red men of America, as well as the most highly civilized nations of modern times in all quarters of the globe. All his words and all his actions, while they were fully adapted to the occasions which called them forth, retain their force and applicability undiminished to all ages and nations. He is the same unsurpassed and unsurpassable model of every virtue to the Christians of every generation, every clime, every sect, every nation, and every race.

---

1. 1 Cor. xi. 1. Comp. 1 Thess. i. 6: "Ye became followers of us and of the Lord."
2. Matt. iv. 19; viii. 22; ix. 9; Mark ii. 14; viii. 84; x. 21; Luke v. 27; ix. 23; 59; xviii. 22; John i. 43; x. 27; xii. 26.
3. Matt. xii. 1-8; Mark ii. 23-28; Luke v. 1-9; John v. 16-18.
4. John ix. 3: "Neither hath this man sinned, nor his parents; (but he was born blind,) that the works of God should be made manifest in him."
5. See the dialogue with the woman of Samaria, John iv. 5 ff.; and the parable of the merciful Samaritan, Luke x. 30-37.

8

HARMONY OF ALL GRACES AND VIRTUES IN CHRIST

IT must not be supposed that a complete catalogue of virtues would do justice to the character under consideration. It is not only the completeness, but still more the even proportion and perfect harmony of virtues and graces apparently opposite and contradictory, which distinguishes him specifically from all other men. This feature gives the finish to that beauty of holiness which is the sublimest picture that can be presented to our contemplation. It has struck with singular force all the more eminent writers on the subject.[1]

Christ was free from all one-sidedness; which constitutes the weakness as well as the strength of the most eminent men. He was not a man of one idea, nor of one virtue towering above all the rest. The moral forces were so well tempered and moderated by each other, that none was unduly prominent, none carried to excess, none alloyed by the kindred failing. Each was checked and completed by the opposite grace. His character never lost its even balance and happy equilibrium, never needed modification or re-adjustment. It was thoroughly sound and uniformly consistent from the beginning t6 the end.

We can not properly attribute to him any one temperament. He was neither sanguine, like Peter; nor choleric, like Paul; nor melancholy, like John; nor phlegmatic, as James is sometimes, though incorrectly, represented to have been: but he combined the vivacity without the

54

levity of the sanguine, the vigor without the violence of the choleric, the seriousness without the austerity of the melancholic, the calmness without the apathy of the phlegmatic, temperament.

He was equally far removed from the excesses of the legalist, the pietist, the ascetic, and the enthusiast. With the strictest obedience to the law, he moved in the element of freedom; with all the fervor of the enthusiast, he was always calm, sober, and self-possessed. Notwithstanding his complete and uniform elevation above the affairs of this world, he fireely mingled with society, male and female, dined with publicans and sinners, played with little children and blessed them, sat at the wedding-feast, shed tears at the sepulcher, delighted in God's nature, admired the beauties of the lilies, and used the occupations of the husbandman for the illustration of the sublimest truths of the kingdom of heaven. His virtue was healthy, manly, vigorous, yet genial, social, and truly human; never austere and repulsive; always in full sympathy with innocent joy and pleasure. He, the purest and holiest of men, provided wine for the wedding-feast; introduced the fatted calf and music and dancing into the picture of welcome of the prodigal son to his father's house; and even provoked the sneer of his adversaries, that he "came eating and drinking," and was a "glutton" and a "winebibber."

His zeal never degenerated into passion, nor his constancy into obstinacy, nor his benevolence into weakness, nor his tenderness into sentimentality. His unworldliness was free from indifference and unsociability, his dignity from pride and presumption, his affability from undue familiarity, his self-denial from moroseness, his temperance from austerity. He combined child-like innocence with manly strength, all-absorbing devotion to God with untiring interest in the welfare of man, tender love to the sinner with uncompromising severity against sin, commanding dignity with winning humility, fearless courage with wise caution, unyielding firmness with sweet gentleness.

He is justly compared with the lion in strength, and with the lamb in meekness. He equally possessed the wisdom of the serpent and the simplicity of the dove. He brought both the sword against every form of wickedness, and the peace which the world can not give. He was the most effective, and yet the least noisy, the most radical, and yet the most conservative, calm, and patient, of all reformers. He came to fulfill every letter of the law; and yet he made all things new. The same hand which drove the profane traffickers from the Temple blessed little children, healed the lepers, and rescued the sinking disciple; the same ear which heard the voice of approbation from heaven was open to the cries of the woman in travail; the same mouth which pronounced the terrible woe on hypocrites, and condemned the impure desire and unkind feeling as well as the open crime, blessed the poor in spirit, announced pardon to the adulteress, and prayed for his murderers; the same eye which beheld the mysteries of God, and penetrated the heart of man, shed tears of compassion over ungrateful Jerusalem, and tears of friendship at the grave of Lazarus.

These are indeed opposite traits of character, yet as little contradictory as the different manifestations of God's power and goodness in the tempest and the sunshine, in the towering Alps and the lily of the valley, in the boundless ocean and the dew-drop of the morning. They are separated in imperfect men indeed, but united in Christ, the universal model for all.

---

1. Comp. Ullmann, "*Sündlosigkeit,*" p. 67; J. P. Lange, "*Leben Jesu,*" i. 27-34; Ebrard, "*Dogmatik,*" vol. ii. 23, 24. Also Hase, in his "*Leben Jesu,*" p. 63 (4th ed.), places the ideal beauty of Christ's character in "*das schöne Ebenmaass aller Kräfte,*" and in "*vollendete Gottesliebe dargestellt in reinster Humanität*" ("The beautiful symmetry of all powers, and perfect love to God, exhibited in purest humanity"). Bishop D. Wilson, in his "*Evidences of Christianity,*" vol. ii. 116 (Boston ed. of 1830), remarks: "The opposite, and to us apparently contradictory, graces were found in Christ in equal proportion." Dr. W. E. Channing, the Unitarian, in his able and remarkable sermon on the "*Character of Christ*" (Works, vol. iv. p. 23), says: "This combination of the spirit of humanity, in its lowliest, tenderest form, with the consciousness of unrivaled and divine glories, is the most wonderful distinction of this wonderful character." Guizot, *Méditations sur l'essence de la relig. chrétienne*, 1864, p. 274: "*Rien ne me frappe plus dans les Évangiles que ce double caractère de sévérité et d'amour, de pureté austère et de sympathie tendre qui apparaît et règne constamment dans les actes et dans les paroles de Jésus-Christ, en tout ce qui touche aux rapports de Dieu avec les hommes.*" I add a testimony from an excellent little apologetic work which has just come to hand,—"*Apologetischle Vorträge über die Grundwahrheiten des Christenthums*, von Dr. Chr. E. Luthardt," Leipz. 1864, p. 204: "The image of Jesus is the ilnage of the highest and purest, *harmony* both of his natural and his

moral being. With all other Inen, there is some discrepancy in the inner life. The two poles of intellectual life, knowledge, and feeling, head and heart; the two powers of the moral life, thought and will,—in whom are they fully agreed?]But as to Jesus, we all have the lively impression, here reigns perfect harmony of the inner spiritual life. His soul is at absolute peace. . . . He is all love, all heart, all feeling; and yet, on the other hand, all intellect, all clearness, all majesty. . . . All is quiet greatness, peaceful simplicity, sublime harmony."

9

HIS PASSION AND CRUCIFIXION

AS all active virtues meet in Jesus, so he unites the active or heroic virtues with the passive and gentle. He is the highest standard of all true martyrdom.

No character can become complete without trial and suffering; and a noble death is the crowning act of a noble life. Edmund Burke said to Fox, in the English Parliament, "Obloquy is a necessary ingredient of all true glory, Calumny and abuse are essential parts of triumph." The ancient Greeks and Romans admired a good man struggling with misfortune, as a sight worthy of the gods. Plato describes the righteous man as one who, without doing any injustice, yet has the appearance of the greatest injustice, and proves his own justice by perseverance against all calumny unto death; yea, he predicts, that, if such a righteous man should ever appear, he would be scourged, tortured, bound, deprived of his sight, and, after having suffered all possible injury, nailed to a post.[1] No wonder that the ancient fathers and modern divines saw in this remarkable passage a striking parallel to the description of Isaiah, ch. liii., and an unconscious prophecy of the suffering Christ. But how far is this abstract ideal of the great philosopher from the actual reality as it appeared three hundred years afterward! The great men of this world, who rise even above themselves on inspiring occasions, and boldly face a superior army, are often thrown off their equilibrium in ordinary life, and grow impatient at trifling obstacles. Only think of Napoleon at the head of his conquering legions and at the helm of an empire, and the same Napoleon after the defeat at Waterloo and on the Island of St. Helena!

The highest form of passive virtue attained by ancient heathenism or modern secular heroism is that stoicism which meets and overcomes the trials and misfortunes of life in the spirit of haughty contempt and unfeeling indifference which destroys the sensibilities, and is but another exhibition of selfishness and pride.

Christ has set up a far higher standard by his teaching and example, never known before or since, except in imperfect imitation of him. He has revolutionized moral philosophy, and convinced the world that forgiving love to the enemy, holiness and humility, gentle patience in suffering, and cheerful submission to the holy will of God, are the crowning excellency of moral greatness. "If thy brother," he says, "trespass against thee seven times in a day, and seven times in a day turn again to thee, saying, I repent; thou shalt forgive him" (Luke xvii. 4). "Love your enemies, bless them that curse you, do good to them that hate you, and pray for them that despitefully use you and persecute you " (Matt. v. 44). This is a sublime maxim truly; but still more sublime is its actual exhibition in his life.

Christ's passive virtue is not confined to the closing scenes of his ministry. As human life is beset at every step with trials, vexatious, and hindrances, which should serve the educational purposes of developing its resources and proving its strength, so was Christ's. During the whole state of his humiliation, he was "a man of sorrows, and acquainted with grief" (Isa. liii. 3), and had to endure the "contradiction of sinners" (Heb. xii. 3). He was poor, and suffered hunger and fatigue; he was tempted by the devil; his path was obstructed with apparently insurmountable difficulties from the outset; his words and miracles called forth the bitter hatred of the world, which resulted at last in the bloody counsel of death. The Pharisees and Sadducees forgot their jealousies and quarrels in opposing him. They rejected and perverted his testimony; they laid snares for him by insidious questions; they called him a glutton and a wine-bibber for eating and drinking like other men; a friend of publicans and sinners for his condescending love and mercy; a Sabbath-breaker for doing good on the Sabbath day: they charged him with madness and blasphemy for asserting his unity with the Father, and derived his miracles from Beelzebub, the prince of devils. The common people, though astonished at his wisdom and mighty works, pointed sneeringly at his origin; his own country and native town refused him the honor of a prophet: even his brothers, we are told, did not believe in him; and, in their impatient zeal for a temporal kingdom, they found fault with his unostentatious mode of proceeding.[2] Even his apostles and disciples, notwithstanding their profound reverence for his character, and faith in his divine origin and mission as the Messiah of God, yet by their ignorance, their carnal Jewish notions, and their almost habitual misunderstanding of his spiritual discourses, must have constituted a severe trial of patience to a teacher of far less superiority to his pupils.

To all this must be added the constant sufferings from sympathy with human misery as it met him in ten thousand forms at every step. What a trial for him, the purest, gentlest, most tender-hearted of men, to breathe more than thirty years the foul atmosphere of this fallen world; to see the constant outbursts of sinful passions; to hear the great wail of humanity borne to his ears upon the four winds of heaven; to be brought into personal contact with the blind, the lame, the deaf, the paralytic, the lunatic, the possessed, the dead; and to be assaulted, as it were, by the concentrated force of sickness, sorrow, grief, and agony!

But how shall we describe his passion, more properly so called, with which no other suffering can be compared for a moment? There is a lonely grandeur in it, foreshadowed in the word of the prophet: "I have trodden the wine-press alone, and of the people there was none with me" (Isa. lxiii. 3). If great men occupy a solitary position, far above the ordinary level, on the sublime hights of thought or action, how much more, then, Jesus in his sufferings,—he, the purest and holiest of beings! The nearer a man approaches to moral perfection, the deeper are his sensibilities, the keener his sense of sin and evil and sorrow in this wicked world.

Never did any man suffer more innocently, more unjustly, more intensely, than Jesus of Nazareth. Within the narrow limits of a few hours, we have here a tragedy of universal significance, exhibiting every form of human weakness and infernal wickedness; of ingratitude, desertion, injury, and insult; of bodily and mental pain and anguish; culminating in the most ignominious death then known among the Jews and Gentiles,—the death of a malefactor and a slave. The government and the people combined against Him who came to save them. His own disciples forsook him; Peter denied him; Judas, under the inspiration of the devil, betrayed him; the rulers of the nation condemned him; rude soldiers mocked him; the furious mob cried, "Crucify him!" He was seized in the night, hurried from tribunal to tribunal, arrayed in a crown of thorns, insulted, smitten, scourged, spit upon, and hung like a criminal and a slave between two robbers and murderers!

How did Christ bear all these little and great trials of life, and the death on the cross?

Let us remember first, that, unlike the icy Stoics in their unnatural and repulsive pseudo-virtue, he had the keenest sensibilities and the deepest sympathies with all human grief, that made him even shed tears at the grave of a friend and in the agony of the garden, and provide a refuge for his mother in the last dying hour. But with this touching tenderness and delicacy of feeling he ever combined an unutterable dignity and majesty, a sublime self-control, and imperturbable calmness of mind. There is a commanding grandeur and majesty in his deepest sufferings, which forbid a feeling of pity and compassion on our side as incompatible with the admiration and deference for his character. We feel the force of his words to the women of Jerusalem, when they bewailed him on the way to Calvary: "Weep not for me, but weep for yourselves and your children." We never hear him break out in angry passion and violence, although he was at war with the whole ungodly world. He clearly and fully foresaw, and repeatedly foretold his sufferings to his disciples.

And yet he never murmured,—never uttered discontent, displeasure, or resentment. He was never disheartened, discouraged, ruffled, or fretted, but full of unbounded confidence that all was well ordered in the providence of his heavenly Father. His calmness in the tempest on the lake, when his disciples were trembling on the brink of destruction and despair, is an illustration of his heavenly frame of mind. All his works were performed with a quiet dignity and ease that contrast most strikingly with the surrounding commotion and excitement. He never asked the favor, or heard the applause, or feared the threat, of the world. He moved serenely, like the sun, above the clouds of human passions and trials and commotions as they sailed under him. He was ever surrounded with the element of peace, even in his parting hour in that dark and solemn night, when he said to his disturbed disciples: "Peace I leave with you, my peace I give unto you; not as the world giveth give I unto you. Let not your heart be troubled, neither let it be afraid" (John xiv. 27). He was never what we call unhappy, but full of inward joy, which he bequeathed to his disciples in that sublimest of all prayers, "that they might have his joy fulfilled in themselves" (John xvii. 13; comp. xvi. 33). With all his severe rebuke to the Pharisees, he never indulged in personalities. He ever returned good for evil. He forgave Peter for his denial; and would have forgiven Judas, if, in the exercise of sincere repentance, he had sought his pardon. Even while hanging on the cross, he had only the language of pity for the wretches who were driving the nails into his hands and feet; and prayed in their behalf: "Father, forgive them; for they know not what they do." He did not seek or hasten his martyrdom, like many of the early martyrs of the Ignatian type, in their morbid enthusiasm and ambitious humility, but quietly and patiently waited for the hour appointed by the will of his heavenly Father.

But, when the hour came, with what self-possession and calmness, with what strength and meekness, with what majesty and gentleness, did he pass through its dark and trying scenes! A prisoner before Pilate, who represented the power of the Roman Empire, he professes himself a king of truth, and makes the governor tremble before him (John xviii. 37; Matt. xxvii. 19, 24). Charged with crime at the tribunal of the high-priest, he speaks to him with the majesty and dignity of the Judge of the world (Matt. xxvi. 64); and in the agony of death on the cross he dispenses a place in paradise to the penitent robber (Luke xxii. 43). In the history of the passion, every word and act are unutterably signifi-cant; from the agony in Gethsemane, when overwhelmed with the sympathetic sense of the entire guilt of mankind, and in full view of the terrible scenes before him,—the only guiltless being in the world,—he prayed that the cup might pass from him, but immediately added: "Not my, but thy, will be done," to the triumphant exclamation on the cross: "It is finished!" Even his dignified silence before the tribunal of his enemies and the furious mob, when, "as a lamb dumb before his shearers, he opened not his mouth," is more eloquent than any apology.

Who will venture to bring a parallel from the annals of ancient or modern sages, when even a Rousseau confessed: "If Socrates suffered and died like a philosopher, Christ suffered and died like a God "?[3] The nearer we approach to them, the more we feel that the sufferings of Christ are unlike any other suffering; that he died the just for the unjust, the Holy One for sinners; and washed out with his blood the guilt of a fallen world. We bow down, and adore the atoning sacrifice of boundless love. The mere idea of a merciful divine-human Redeemer of the race from the thralldom of misery and of sin and death, is surpassingly sublime and irresistibly attractive: how much more the actual reality! It is, indeed, a mystery which we can not fully grasp; but a mystery so palpably divine and heavenly in its origin and character, so blessed in its effects, that head and heart are constrained to bow in adoration and praise, and are filled with gratitude and joy. The passion and crucifixion of Jesus, like his whole character, stand without a parallel, solitary and alone in their glory, and will ever continue to be what they have been for these eighteen hundred years,—the most sacred theme of meditation, the highest exemplar of suffering virtue, the strongest weapon against sin and Satan, the deepest source of comfort to the noblest and best of men.

---

1. "*Politia,*" p. 74 sq. ed. Ast. ("*Plat. Opera,*" vol. iv. p. 360, E. ed. Bip.) Compare, the author's "*History of the Apostolic Church,*" English edition, § 109, page 433 f. Even Jean Jacques Rousseau was struck with this remarkable heathen prophecy of the suffering Saviour, who died the death of a malefactor and a slave to redeem us. "*Quand Platon,*" he says in his "*Émil,*" "*peint son juste imaginaire couvert de tout l'opprobre du crime et digne de tous les prix de la vertu, il peint trait pour trait Jésus Christ: la ressemblance est si frappante, que tous les pères l'ont sentie, et qu'il n'est pas possible de s'y tromper.*"
2. John vii. 3-10. It is immaterial for our purpose whether we understand by his brothers (not "brethren," as the Common Version has it) younger sons of Joseph

and Mary, or older sons of Joseph from a former marriage, or cousins of Jesus. They appear, at all events, as members and inmates of the holy family either by birth or adoption. Compare the author's exegetical article on the *"Brothers of Christ,"* in the *"Bibliotheca Sacra"* for October, 1864; and notes in his edition of Lange's *"Commentary on Matthew,"* p. 256 if.

3. Rousseau, *"Émil,"* iv. p. 111: *"Oui, si la vie et la mort de Socrate sont d'un sage; la vie et la mort de Jésus sont d'un dieu!"*

10

SUMMARY

CHRIST'S CHARACTER THE GREATEST MORAL MIRACLE OF HISTORY.

SUCH was Jesus of Nazareth,—a true man in body, soul, and spirit, yet differing from all men; a character absolutely unique and original from tender childhood to ripe manhood, moving in unbroken union with God, overflowing with the purest love to man, free from every sin and error, innocent and holy, teaching and practicing all virtues in perfect harmony, devoted solely and uniformly to the noblest ends, sealing the purest life with the sublimest death, and ever acknowledged since as the one and only perfect model of goodness and holiness! All human greatness loses on closer inspection; but Christ's character grows more pure, sacred, and lovely, the better we know him. The whole range of history and fiction furnishes no parallel to it. There never was any thing even approaching to it, before or since, except in faint imitation of his example.

No biographer, moralist, or artist can be satisfied with any attempt of his to set forth the beauty of holiness which shines from the face of Jesus of Nazareth. It is felt to be infinitely greater than any conception or representation of it by the mind, the tongue, or the pencil of man or angel. We might as well attempt to empty the waters of the boundless sea into a narrow well, or to portray the splendor of the risen sun and the starry heavens with ink. No picture of the Saviour, though drawn by the master hand of a Raphael or Dürer or Rubens; no epic, though conceived by the genius of a Dante or Milton or Klopstock,—can improve on the artless, narrative of the Gospels, whose only but all-powerful charm is truth. In this case, certainly, truth is stranger than fiction, and speaks best for itself without comment, explanation, or eulogy. Here, and here alone, the highest perfection of art falls short of the historical fact, and fancy finds no room for idealizing the real; for here we have the absolute ideal itself in living reality. It seems to me that this consideration alone should satisfy any reflecting mind that Christ's character, though truly natural and human, rises far above the ordinary proportions of humanity, and can not be classified with the purest and greatest of our race.

This conviction has forced itself more or less clearly even upon some opponents of Christianity, and many of the greatest worldly intellects, in proportion as they allowed themselves to yield to the light of truth and the power of facts. Jean Jacques Rousseau, one of the leaders of French infidelity in the eighteenth century, admitted, in his "*Émile*," that there could be no comparison between Socrates and Christ; as little as between a sage and a God. Napoleon, though a perfect stranger to religion in his heart, saw with his keen eagle-eye that Christ was more than man; and that, once admitting his divinity, the Christian system becomes as clear and precise as a problem of algebra. I refer, of course, to his remarkable utterances on this subject at St. Helena, which may have been somewhat modified and expanded, but bear the unmistakable evidence of the Napoleonic grasp and style. Goethe, the most universal and finished, but at the same time the most worldly and self-sufficient, of all modern poets, calls Christ "the Divine Man," "the Holy One," and represents him as the pattern and model of humanity. Jean Paul Frederick Richter, the greatest of German humorists, pays this homage of genius to Jesus of Nazareth: "He is the purest among the mighty, the mightiest among the pure, who with his pierced hand has raised empires from their foundations, turned the stream of history from its old channel, and still continues to rule and guide the ages."[1] Thomas Carlyle, the British hero-worshiper, found no equal in all the range of ancient and modern heroism. He calls his life a "perfect ideal poem," and his person "the greatest of all heroes," whom he does not name, leaving "sacred silence to meditate that sacred matter." Ernest

Renan, the famous French orientalist and critic, who views Jesus from the stand-point of a Pantheistic naturalism, and expels all miracles from the gospel-history, feels constrained to call him "a man of colossal dimensions;" "the incomparable man, to whom the universal conscience has decreed the title of *Son of God,* and that with justice, since he caused religion to take a step in advance incomparably greater than any other in the past, and probably than *any yet to come*;" and he closes his "Life of Jesus" with the remarkable concession: "Whatever may be the surprises of the future, *Jesus will never be surpassed.* His worship will grow young without ceasing; his legend will call forth tears without end; his sufferings will melt the noblest hearts; all ages will proclaim, that, among the sons of men, there is none born greater than Jesus."[2] Dr. Baur, the teacher of Strauss, the master of the modern critical school, and the ablest and most earnest scholar among all modern heretics and infidels, came to the conclusion at last, after all the critical investigations of a long and intensely studious life, that the person of Christ remains a great mystery in history; and that, at all events, the whole world-historical significance of Christianity hangs on his person.[3]

Yes: Christ's person is, indeed, a great but blessed mystery. It can not be explained on purely humanitarian principles, nor derived from any intellectual and moral forces of the age in which he lived. On the contrary, it stands in marked contrast to the whole surrounding world of Judaism and Heathenism, which presents to us the dreary picture of internal decay, and which actually crumbled into ruin before the new moral creation of the crucified Jesus of Nazareth. He is the one absolute and unaccountable exception to the universal experience of mankind. He is the great central miracle of the whole gospel-history. All his miracles are but the natural and necessary manifestations of his miraculous person, and hence they were performed with the same ease with which we perform our ordinary daily works. In the Gospel of St. John, they are simply and justly called his "works." It would be the greatest miracle indeed, if He, who is a miracle himself, should have performed no miracles.

Here is just the logical inconsistency, contradiction, and absurdity of those unbelievers who admit the extraordinary character of Christ's person, and yet deny his extraordinary works. They admit a cause without a corresponding effect, and involve the person in conflict with his works, or the works with the person. You may as well expect the sun to send forth darkness as to expect ordinary works from such an extraordinary being.

The person of Christ accounts for all the wonderful phenomena in his history, as a sufficient cause for the effect. Such a power over the soul as he possessed, and still exercises from day to day throughout Christendom,—why should it not extend also over the lesser sphere of the body? What was it for him, who is spiritually the Resurrection and the Life of the race, to call forth a corpse from the grave? Could such a heavenly life and heavenly death as his end in any other way than in absolute triumph over death, and in ascension to heaven, its proper origin and home?

The supernatural and miraculous in Christ, let it be borne in mind, was not a borrowed gift or an occasional manifestation, as we find it among the prophets and apostles, but an inherent power in constant silent or public exercise. An inward virtue dwelt in his person, and went forth from him, so that even the fringe of his garment was healing to the touch through the medium of faith which is the bond of union between him and the soul. He was the true Shekinah, and shone in all his glory, not before the multitude or the unbelieving Pharisees and scribes, but when he was alone with his Father, or walked in the dark night over the waves of the sea, calming the storm of nature and strengthening the faith of his timid disciples, or when he stood between Moses and Elijah before his favorite three on the mount of transfiguration.

Thus from every direction we arrive at the conclusion, that Christ, though truly natural and human, was at the same time truly supernatural and divine. The wonderful character of his person forces upon us the inevitable admission of the indwelling of the Divinity in him, as the only rational and satisfactory explanation of this mysterious fact; and this is the explanation which he gives himself.

---

1. "Der Reinste unter den Mächtigen, der Mächtigste unter den Reinen, der mit

seiner durchstochenen Hand Reiche aus der Angel, den Strom der Jahrhunderte aus dem Bette hob und noch fortgebietet den Zeiten." Jean Paul: *"Ueber den Gott in der Geschichte und im Leben." Sämmtliche Werke,* vol. xxxiii. 6.

2. *"Vie de Jésus,"* 7th ed. Paris, 1864, p. 325: *"Quels que puissent être les phénomènes inattendues de l'avenir, Jésus ne sera pas surpassé. Son culte se rajeunira sans cesse; sa légende provoquera des larmes sans fin; ses souffrances atteindront les meilleurs cœurs; tous les siècles proclameront qu'entre les fils des hommes, il n'en est pas né de plus grand que Jésus."* Renan, however, spoils all his concessions, which are quite frequent and enthusiastic, by his pantheistic man-worship, and by placing such a comparatively obscure individual as Cakya-Mouni, or Saint Sakya, the founder of Buddhism, on a par with Christ. Compare the last chapter of his *"Vie de Jésus,"* and also the conclusion of his essay on the *"Critical Historians of Jesus,"* where he says of Christ: "The wonder-worker and the prophet will die; the man and the sage will endure; or, rather, the eternal beauty will live for ever in this sublime name, as in all those whom humanity has chosen to keep it in mind of its own nature, and to transport it by the view of its own image. Behold there the living God! This is the adorable One!"

3. Dr. Baur: *"Das Christenthum und die christliche Kirche der drei ersten Jahrhunderte,"* second revised edition, which appeared shortly before his death (1860), p. 53 f. The resurrection especially remained for Dr. Baur an unsolved problem; and this fact is the very foundation on which the Christian Church is built, and has ever since defied the gates of hell.

11

CHRIST'S OWN TESTIMONY CONCERNING HIMSELF

THERE is but one rational explanation, of this sublime mystery; and this is found in Christ's own testimony concerning his superhuman and divine origin and character.[1] This testimony challenges at once our highest regard and belief from the absolute veracity which no one ever denied him, or could deny, without destroying at once the very foundation of his universally conceded moral purity and greatness.

Christ strongly asserts his humanity, and calls himself; about eighty times in the Gospels, *the Son of man*.[2] This expression, while it places him in one view on common ground with us as flesh of our flesh, and bone of our bone, already indicates at the same time that he is more than an ordinary individual,—not merely *a* son of man like all other descendants of Adam, but *the* Son of man; the Man in the highest sense; the ideal, the universal, the absolute Man; the second Adam, descended from heaven; the Head of a new and superior order of the race, the King of Israel, the Messiah.[3] The same is the case substantially, though less clearly, with the cognate term, "the Son of David," which is frequently given to Christ as an official title of the promised Messiah, the King of Israel, as by the two blind men, the Syrophenician woman, and the people at large.[4]

The appellation *the Son of man* does not express, then, as many suppose, the humiliation and condescension of Christ simply, but his elevation rather above the ordinary level, and the actualization, in him and through him, of the ideal standard of human nature under its moral and religious aspect, or in its relation to God. This interpretation is suggested grammatically by the use of the definite article, and historically by the origin of the term in Dan. vii. 13, where it signifies the Messiah, as the head of a universal and eternal kingdom. It commends itself, moreover, at once as the most natural and significant, in such passages as, "Ye shall see the heavens open, and the angels of God ascending and descending upon the Son of man" (John i. 51); "He that came down from heavens even the Son of man which is in heaven" (John iii. 13); "The Son of man hath power to forgive sins" (Matt. ix. 6; Mark ii. 10); "The Son of man is Lord even of the Sabbath day" (Matt. xii. 8; Mark ii. 28); "Except ye eat the flesh of the Son of man, and drink his blood, ye have no life in you" (John vi. 53); "The Son of man shall come in the glory of his Father;"[5] "The Son of man is come to save " (Matt. xviii. 11; comp. Luke xix. 10); "The Father hath given him authority to execute judgment also, because he is the Son of man" (John v. 27). Even those passages which are quoted for the opposite view, receive, in our interpretation, a greater force and beauty from the sublime contrast which places the voluntary condescension and humiliation of Christ in the most striking light, as when he says: "Foxes have holes, and birds of the air have nests; but the Son of man hath not where to lay his head" (Luke ix. 58): or, "Whosoever will be chief among you, let him be your servant; even as the Son of man came not to be ministered unto, but to minister, and to give his life a ransom for many" (Matt. xx. 27, 28). Thus the manhood of Christ, rising far above all ordinary manhood, though freely coming down to its lowest ranks with the view to their elevation and redemption, is already the portal of his Godhood.

But he calls himself at the same time, as he is most frequently called by his disciples, *the Son of God*, in an equally emphatic sense. He is not merely a son of God among others,—angels, archangels, princes and judges and redeemed men,—but *the* Son of God as no other being ever was, is, or can be; all others being sons or children of God only by derivation or adoption, after a new spiritual birth, and in dependence on his absolute and eternal Sonship.[6] He is, as his favorite disciple calls him, the *only-begotten Son*, or, as the old catholic theology expresses it, "eternally begotten of the substance of the Father." In this high sense the title is freely given to him by his disciples,[7] without a remonstrance on his part; and by God, the Father himself, at his baptism and at the transfiguration.[8] It is significant too, that, while he directs us to address God as "*our* Father," he himself always addresses him: "*My* Father," because he sustains a peculiar relation to him far above the level of human children of God, who are made such only by regeneration and adoption.

Christ founds his whole doctrine and kingdom on his own person. His divine-human person is his constant theme, his cause. He is himself the gospel. All this he does without the remotest sense of pride or ambition or vanity, but with the simplicity and authority of self-evident truth. Hence his words have such an overwhelming power over the hearts. "Verily, verily, I say unto you." So God speaks in the Old Testament, but no man. "If ye believe not that I am he, ye shall die in your sins " (John viii. 24). What a majesty is implied in this declaration!

Christ represents himself constantly as being "not of this world," but "sent from God," as having "come from God," and as "being in heaven" while living on earth (John iii. 13). He not only announces and proclaims the truth as other messengers of God, but declares himself to be "the Light of the World" (John viii. 12); "the Way, the Truth, and the Life" (John xiv. 6); "the Resurrection and the Life" (John xi. 25). "All things," he says, "are delivered unto me of my Father; and no man knoweth the Son but the Father; neither knoweth any man the Father save the Son, and he to whomsoever the Son will reveal him."[9] He invites the weary and heavy-laden to come to him for rest and peace (Matt. xi. 28); he promises life in the highest and deepest sense, even eternal life, to every one who believes in him;[10] he claims and admits himself to be the Christ, or the Messiah, of whom Moses and the prophets of old testify, and the King of Israel.[11] When, in view of his approaching death, and under a solemn appeal to the living God, he was challenged by the Jewish high priest, in the name of the venerable though corrupt theocracy, with the question: "Art thou the Christ (the promised Messiah), the Son of God?" he calmly and deliberately answered in the affirmative, and pointed him to his glorious return in the clouds of heaven; thus proclaiming himself, in the moment of the deepest humiliation and in the face of the apparent triumph of the powers of darkness, the God-like Ruler and Judge of mankind![12]

The only choice here is between a truly divine man and a mad blasphemer. The high priest understood the meaning of this solemn affirmation better than many modern commentators: he rent his sacerdotal garment, and exclaimed in indignation and horror: "Thou hast spoken blasphemy!"

Jesus, moreover, repeatedly represents himself as the Lawgiver of. the new and last dispensation (Matt. v. 22-24; xxviii. 19, 20); as the Founder of a spiritual kingdom co-extensive with the race, and everlasting as eternity itself;[13] as the appointed Judge of the quick and the dead;[14] as the only Mediator between God and man; as the Saviour of the world.[15] He parts from his disciples with those sublime words, which alone certify his divinity: "All power is given to me in heaven and in earth. Go ye, therefore, and teach all nations, baptizing them in the name of the Father, and of the Son, and of the Holy Ghost; teaching them to observe all things whatsoever I have commanded you: and, lo, I am with you alway, even to the end of the world" (Matt. xxviii. 18-20).

Finally, he claims such a relation to the Father as implies both the equality of substance and the distinction of person, and which, in connection with his declarations concerning the Holy Spirit, leads with. logical necessity, as it were, to the doctrine of the Holy Trinity. For this doctrine alone saves the divinity of Christ and of the Holy Spirit, without affecting the fundamental truth of the Unity of the Godhead; and keeps the proper medium between an abstract and lifeless monotheism and a polytheistic tritheism.

Christ always distinguishes himself from God the Father, who sent him, whose works he came to fulfill, whose will he obeys, by whose power he performs his miracles, to whom he prays, and with whom he communes, as a self-conscious personal being. And so lie distinguishes himself with equal clearness from the Holy Spirit, whom he received at his baptism, whom he breathed into his disciples, and whom he promised to send and did send on them as the other Paraclete, as the Spirit of truth and holiness, with the whole fullness of the accomplished salvation. But he never makes a similar distinction between himself and the Son of God: on the contrary, he identifies himself with the Son of God, and uses this term, as already remarked, in a sense which implies much more than the Jewish conception of the Messiah, and nothing short of the equality of essence or substance.

For he claims, as the Son, a real, self-conscious pre-existence before man, and even before the world: consequently, also, before time; for time was created with the world.[16] Hence the Arian notion of a *temporal* preexistence of Christ is metaphysically untenable. It assumes a creature to have existed before the creation, and a finite being to have begun existence before time. Before the act of creation, there was nothing but God and eternity. Time is the necessary form under which the world exists successively, as space is the form under which all material substances exist simultaneously. Time, before the world, could only have referred to God, who does not exist in time, but in eternity. "*Before* Abraham *was*," or *began to be*, says Christ, "I *am*;" significantly using the past tense in the one and the present in the other case to mark the difference between man's temporal and his own eternal mode of existence.[17] In the sacerdotal prayer, he asks to be clothed again with the glory which he *had* with the Father *before* the foundation of the world.[18] He assumes divine names and attributes as far as consistent with his state of humiliation; he demands and receives divine honors (John v. 23); he freely and repeatedly exercises the prerogative of pardoning sin in his own name, which the unbelieving scribes and Pharisees, with a logic whose force is irresistible on their premises, looked upon as blasphemous presumption;[19] he familiarly classes himself with the infinite majesty of Jehovah in one common plural, and boldly declares: "He that hath seen me hath seen the Father" (John xiv. 9); "I and the Father are one" (John x. 30).[20] He co-ordinates himself, in the baptismal formula, with the Divine Father and the Divine Spirit (Matt. xxviii. 19); and allows himself to be called by Thomas, in the name of all the apostles, "My Lord and my God!" (John xx. 28.)

These are the most astounding and transcendent pretensions ever set up by any being. He, the humblest and lowliest of men, makes them repeatedly and uniformly to the last, in the face of the whole world,—even in the darkest hour of suffering. He makes them, not in swelling, pompous, ostentatious language, which almost necessarily springs from false pretensions, but in a natural, spontaneous style, with perfect ease, freedom, and composure, as a native prince would speak of the attributes and scenes of royalty at his father's court. He never falters or doubts, never apologizes for them, never enters into an explanation: he sets them forth as self-evident truths, which need only be stated to challenge the belief and submission of mankind.

Now, suppose for a moment a purely human teacher, however great and good; suppose a Moses or Elijah, a John the Baptist, an Apostle Paul, or John,—not to speak of any church-father, schoolman, or reformer,—to say: "I am the Light of the world;" "I am the Way, the Truth, and the Life;" "I and the Father are one;" and to call upon all men, "Come unto me;" "Follow me," that you may find "life" and "peace," which you can not find elsewhere: would it not create a universal feeling of pity or indignation? No human being on earth could set up the least of these pretensions, without being set down at once as a madman or a blasphemer.[21]

But from the mouth of Christ these colossal pretensions excite neither pity nor indignation, nor even the least feeling of incongruity or impropriety. We read and hear them over and over again without surprise.[22] They seem perfectly natural, and well sustained by the most extraordinary life and the most extraordinary works. There is no room here for the least suspicion of vanity, pride, or self-deception. For these eighteen hundred years, these claims have been acknowledged by millions of people of all nations and tongues, of all classes and conditions, of the most learned and mighty as well. as the most ignorant and humble, with an instinctive sense of the perfect agreement of what Christ claimed to be with what he really was.

Is not this fact most remarkable? Is it not a triumphant vindication of Christ's character, and an irresistible proof of the truth of his pretensions? And can we deny the truth, and refuse to acknowledge his divinity, without destroying his veracity, and overthrowing the very foundation of his moral goodness and purity, as universally acknowledged even by heretics and unbelievers? If he, the wisest, the best, the holiest of men, the greatest teacher and benefactor of the race,—acknowledged as such by the common consent of the civilized world,—declares himself one with the Father, and so identifies himself in will and aim, in essence and attributes, with the infinite God, to an extent and in a sense as no man or angel or archangel could do for a moment, without blasphemy or insanity, and if *he* receives the divine adoration fro-m his own intimate disciples, how can we, in logical consistency, as well as in harmony with the deepest moral and religious instincts of our nature, refuse to fall down before him, and, with Thomas,—the representative of honest, truth-loving skepticism among his disciples,—to exclaim from the depths of our soul: "My Lord and my God"?

This is the "*testimonium animæ naturaliter Christianæ,*" to use a celebrated expression of Tertullian. It is the testimony of the soul which is originally made for Christ, and longs for him, and finds no satisfaction of its infinite desires for truth, beauty, and goodness, until it believes in Christ,—the Way, the Truth, and the Life, the divine Man and the incarnate God in one undivided person for ever.

---

1. For a very full exposition of this testimony, we refer to the instructive and able work of W. Fr. Gess: "*Die Lehre von der Person Christs entwickelt aus dem Sebstbewusstsein Christi und aus dem Zeugnisse der Apostel.*" Basel. 1856. Dr. Bushnell's admirable essay on the character of Jesus is defective here. He does not establish the proper divinity of Christ, but seems content with the proof that he was more than man, and can not be classified with men. Having carried the reader over the great difficulty, and beyond the boundary of Humanitarianism, he leaves him to his own conclusion concerning the merits of the orthodox view of Christ.
2. Compare the dictionaries, and especially Schmid's and Bruder's Greek, or Bagster's *English Concordance of the New Testament* (the latter republished by the Harpers, New York, 1855), *sub verbo* υἱὸς τοῦ ἀνθρώπου.
3. So many modern German commentators, and also Dr. Trench, who remarks: "He was '*Son of man,*' as alone realizing all which in the idea of man was contained, as the second Adam, the head and representative of the race,—the one true and perfect flower, which ever unfolded itself, of the root and stock of humanity. Claiming this title as his own, he witnessed against opposite poles of error concerning his person,—the Ebionite, to which the exclusive use of the title 'Son of David' might have led; and the Gnostic, which denied the reality of the human nature that bore it" ("*Notes on the Parables,*" ninth London edition, p. 84). Philo,

the Jewish divine and philosopher, a contemporary of Christ, calls the Logos (the eternal Word) the true man, ὁ ἀληθινὸς ἄνθρωπος.

4. Matt. ix. 27; xv. 22; xii23; xxi. 9; xxii. 41 ff., &c.

5. Matt. xvi. 17; compare xix 28; xxiv. 30; xxv. 31; xxvi. 64; Luke xxi. 27, 36.

6. Matt. xi. 27; xxi. 37; xxii 42; xxvi. 63 f.; xxvii. 43; Mark xii. 6; xiii. 32; xiv 62; Luke x. 22; John v. 19-26; ix. 35-38; x. 36; xi. 4; xiv. 13; xvii. 1; xix. 7.

7. Matt. xvi. 16; Mark iii. 11; John i. 18, 34, 49; xi. 27; xx. 31,—besides the many passages in the Acts and Epistles, where the term υἱὸς τοῦ Θεοῦ is as frequent as the term υἱὸς τοῦ ἀνθρώπου in the Gospels.

8. Matt. iii. 17; Luke iii. 22; Matt. xvii. 5; Luke ix. 35.

9. Matt. xi. 27. This passage is a striking parallel to the sublimest sayings in the fourth Gospel, and proves the essential identity of the Synoptist and Johannean picture of Christ. Comp. Lange's "*Commentary on Matthew*," Amer. ed. p. 213.

10. John iii. 36; v. 24; vi. 40, 47, 50-58; xi. 25.

11. John iv. 26; v. 39, 36; Matt. xiv. 33; xvi. 16 f.; xxvi. 63 f., &c.

12. Matt. xxvi. 63-65. Schleiermacher pronounces this affirmative *Yea* of Christ, in view of the surrounding circumstances, the greatest word ever spoken by any man, the most glorious apotheosis, and the most certain assurance by which any divinity could proclaim itself ("*das grösste Wort, was je ein Sterblicher gesagt hat, die herrlichste Apotheose; keine Gottheit kann gewisser sein als die, welche so sich selbst verkündiget*"). See his youthful work, "*Discourses on Religion*" (*Reden über die Religion*), 4th edition, Berlin, 1831, pages 292 and 293. Compare also the remarks of Luthardt, "*Apologetische Vorträge*," p. 213 f.

13. Matt. xvi. 19; xxvii. 11; Luke xxii. 30; John xviii. 36. Comp. Dan. vii. 13; Luke i. 33.

14. John v. 22, 25-27; Matt. xxv. 31 ff., &c.

15. Matt. xviii. 11; Luke ix. 56; xix. 10; John iii. 17; v. 34; x. 9; xii. 47. Compare Luke i. 47; ii. 11; John iv. 42, &c.

16. "*Mundus non factus est in tempore, sed cum tempore.*"

17. John viii. 58: ἀμὴν, ἀμὴν [the solemn announcement of an important truth] λέγω ὑμῖν, πρὶν Ἀβραὰμ γενέσθαι ἐγὼ εἰμί. Mark also the difference of the verb (which is lost in our English version), besides the difference of the tense. For γίνεσθαι, *to become, werden, to begin to be, to pass from non-existence into existence*, implies origin in time or previous non-existence, and is applicable only to created beings; while εἶναι is equally applicable to God and eternal existence. Compare the ἦν of the Λόγος (John i. 1) with the ἐγένετο of the man John, ver. 6. H. A. W. Meyer, the best grammatical commentator now living, correctly remarks on John viii. 58 (pages 249, 250): "*Da Abraham nicht präexistist hatte, sondern (durch seine Geburt) zur Existenz kam, so steht γενέσθαι, wogegen mit εἰμὶ das Sein an sich gemeint ist, welches bei Jesu (sofern er nach seinem göttlichen Wesen vorzeitlich war) ohne vorgängiges Gewordensein war. Das Praesens bezeichnet das aus der Vergangenheit her Fortdauernde. Vrgl.* lxx. Jer. xxi. 5; Ps. xc. 2; *Winer, Gramm.* p. 309." Meyer then goes on to refute the Socinian and rationalistic misinterpretations of the passage.

18. John xvii. 5. Comp. the testimony of the apostles on the pre-existence,—John i. 1-14; Col. i. 16; Heb. i. 2, 3.

19. Matt. ix. 6; Luke v. 20-24; vii. 47, 48.

20. John x. 30. The passage teaches, certainly, more than the ethical unity of will: it asserts, according to the context, the unity of power which is based on the unity of essence, or the homousia. The ἓν excludes Arianism; the plural ἐσμέν, Sabellianism and Patripassianism.

21. Dr. Hengstenberg, in his *"Commentary on the Gospel of St. John,"* 1863, vol. iii. p. 361 f., justly remarks: *"Menschen, die sich selbst zu Gott machen, sind immer entweder Verrückte oder Bösewichter. Wer anders als wer selbst ein Frevler ist, wird es wagen Jesum in die eine oder die andere dieser Classen zu setzen?"*—i.e., men who pretend to be God are always either mad or wicked.

22. "Of all the readers of the gospel," says Bushnell, p. 290, "it probably never even occurs to one in a hundred thousand to blame his conceit, or the egregious vanity of his pretensions." Even the better class of Unitarians instinctively bow before these claims. See the remarkable passage of Dr. Channing quoted below.

EXAMINATION OF FALSE THEORIES

THERE is no other solution of the mighty problem within the reach of
t human learning and ingenuity.

All the infidel and semi-infidel theories of Christ's person substitute an unnatural wonder in the place of the supernatural miracle which
they endeavor to escape. The falsehood of Christ's testimony
concerning himself, as understood and accepted by the universal belief
of Christendom, is not only a mightier wonder than the truth of the
same, but a moral absurdity and monstrosity. Hume says, in his famous
"Essay on Miracles:" "When any one tells me that he saw a dead man
restored to life, I immediately consider with myself, whether it be more
probable that this person should either deceive or be deceived, or that
the fact he relates should really have happened. I weigh the one miracle
against the other; and, according to the superiority which I discover, I
pronounce my decision, and always reject the greater miracle. If the
falsehood of his testimony would be more miraculous than the event
which he relates, then, and not till then, can he pretend to demand my
belief or opinion." We need not fear this test, and can turn it in our case
against Hume and against every doubter of the great miracle of Christ's
person.

Let us briefly review, in detail, the various attempts of Unitarians and unbelievers to account for the character of Christ without admitting his divinity.

1

THE UNITARIAN THEORY.

CHANNING.

The semi-infidelity of the older Socinians and modern Unitarians is singularly inconsistent. Admitting the faultless perfection of Christ's character, and the truthfulness of the gospel-history, including the miracles, and yet denying his divinity, they must either charge him with such egregious exaggerations and conceit as would overthrow at once their concession of his moral perfection, or they must so weaken and pervert his testimony. concerning his relation to God as to violate all the laws of grammar and sound interpretation.

Dr. W. E. Channing, the ablest and noblest representative of modern Unitarianism, prefers to avoid the difficulty which he was unable to solve. In his admirable discourse on the "Character of Christ," he goes as far almost as any orthodox divine in vindicating to him the highest possible purity and excellency as a man; but he stops half-way, and passes by in silence those extraordinary claims which are inexplicable on merely humanitarian and Socinian principles. He approaches, however, the very threshold of the true faith in the following remarkable passage, which we have a right to quote against his own system: "I confess," he says, "when I can escape the deadening power of habit, and can receive the full import of such passages as the following,—'Come unto me, all ye that labor and are heavy

81

laden, and I will give you rest;' 'I am come to seek and to save that which was lost;' 'He that confesseth me before men, him will I confess before my Father in heaven;' 'Whosoever shall be ashamed of me before men, of him shall the Son of man be ashamed when he cometh in the glory of the Father with the holy angels;' 'In my Father's house are many mansions; I go to prepare a place for you:' I say, when I can succeed in realizing the import of such passages, I feel myself listening to a being such as never before and never since spoke in human language. I am awed by the consciousness of greatness which these simple words express; and, when I connect this greatness with the proofs of Christ's miracles which I gave you in a former discourse, I am compelled to exclaim with the centurion: 'Truly, this was the Son of God.'"[1]

But this is not all. We have seen that Christ goes much farther than in the passages here quoted; that he forgives sins in his own name; that he asserts pre-existence before Abraham and before the world, not only ideally in the mind of God,—for this would not distinguish him from Abraham or any other creature,—but in the real sense of self-conscious personal existence; that he claims and receives strictly divine attributes and honors, and makes himself equal with the great Jehovah. How can a being so pure and holy, and withal so humble and lowly, so perfectly free from every trace of enthusiasm and conceit, as Dr. Channing freely and emphatically asserts Christ to have been, lay claim to any thing which he was not in fact? Why, then, not also go beyond the exclamation of the heathen centurion, and unite with the confession of St. Peter and the adoration of the skeptical St. Thomas: "My Lord and my God"?[2] Dr. Channing rose indeed to the high Arian view of Christ in admitting his pre-existence before the world, yet denying his eternity. But this notion involves the metaphysical absurdity of a creature before creation, or of a temporal being before time; for time and world were made together, and are inseparable.

Unitarianism admits altogether too much for its own conclusions, and is therefore driven to the logical alternative of falling back upon an infidel, or of advancing to the orthodox, Christology. Theodore Parker felt this, and gave up the supernatural altogether. Channing, who was certainly under the influence of the holy example of Christ, inclined to the other alternative, as we may infer from his general spirit, and from his last address, delivered at Lenox, Mass., in 1842, shortly before his death, where he said: "The doctrine of the Word made flesh shows us God uniting himself intimately with our nature, manifesting himself' in a human form, for the very end of making us partakers of his own perfection."

---

1. Discourse on the "*Character of Christ*," in Channing's Works, vol. iv. p. 20.
2. The explanation which some Unitarian divines give of these words of Thomas, by resolving them into a mere exclamation of surprise at the fact of the resurrection, "O my God!" is simply absurd, and only worthy of notice as revealing the inextricable difficulty which it presents to the Unitarian Christology.

2

THE HYPOTHESIS OF IMPOSTURE.

REIMARUS.

The infidelity of the enemies of Christianity, which denies the supernatural and miraculous altogether, is logically more consistent than Arianism, Socinianism, and modern Unitarianism, but absolutely untenable in the premises. It resorts either to IMPOSTURE, or ENTHUSIASM, or POETICAL FICTION. These are the only possible hypotheses; which may, however, assume various modifications; and their refutation leaves us no alternative but either absolute skepticism,—which gives up the problem, and ends in nihilism and despair,—or a return to the old and time-honored faith of the Christian Church of all ages.

The hypothesis of imposture is so revolting to moral as well as common sense, that its mere statement is its condemnation. It has never been seriously carried out, and no scholar of any decency and self-respect would now dare to profess it openly.[1] How, in the name of logic, common sense, and experience, could an impostor—that is, a deceitful, selfish, depraved man—have invented, and consistently maintained from beginning to end, the purest and noblest character known in history with the most perfect air of truth and reality? How could he have conceived, and successfully carried through, in the face of the strongest prejudices of his people and age, a plan of unparalleled

84

beneficence, moral magnitude and sublimity, and sacrificed his own life for it?

The difficulty is not lessened by shifting the charge of fraud from Christ upon the apostles and evangelists; for they were any thing but designing hypocrites and deceivers, and leave upon every unsophisticated reader the irresistible impression of an artless simplicity and honesty rarely equaled and never surpassed by any writers, learned or unlearned, of ancient or modern times. What imaginable motive could have induced them to engage in such a wicked scheme, when they knew that the whole world would persecute them even to death? How could they have formed and successfully sustained a conspiracy for such a purpose, without ever falling out, or betraying themselves by some inconsistent word or act?

And who can seriously believe, for a moment, that the Christian Church for these eighteen hundred years, now embracing nearly the whole civilized world, and among them the strongest intellects and the noblest hearts, the greatest divines, philosophers, poets, orators, statesmen, and benefactors of the race, could have been duped and fooled by a Galilean carpenter or a dozen illiterate fishermen?

Verily, this lowest form of infidelity is the grossest insult to all sound reason and sense, and to the dignity of human nature.

---

1. Is was first suggested by the heathen assailants of Christianity, Celsus and Julian the Apostate, then insinuated by French deists of the school of Voltaire, but never raised to the dignity of scientific argument. The only attempt to carry it out, and that a mere fragmentary one, was made by the anonymous "*Wolfenbüttel Fragmentist*," since known as Hermann Samuel Reimrus, professor of Oriental Literature in the College at Hamburg, who died in 1786. His "*Fragments*" were never intended for publication, but only for a few friends. Lessing found them in the library at Wolfenbüttel, and commenced to publish them, without the author's knowledge, in 1774; not, as he said, because he agreed with them, but because he wished to arouse the spirit of investigation. This mode of procedure, Semler, the father of German neology, wittily compared to the act of setting a city on fire for the purpose of trying the engines. In our own time, Bruno Bauer, a theological weathercock, vagabond, and final apostate (not to be confounded with the far superior Dr. F. Ch. Baur), has endeavored to revive, but without effect, this exploded theory, and misrepresented the Gospels as deliberate fabrications. But even Strauss ignores him (in his new "*Life of Jesus*"), as unfit for his company.

3

THE THEORY OF ENTHUSIASM OR SELF-DECEPTION.

The hypothesis of enthusiasm or self-deception, though less disreputable, is equally unreasonable, in view of the uniform clearness, calmness, self-possession, humility, dignity, and patience of Christ,—qualities the very opposite of those which characterize an enthusiast. We might imagine a Jew of that age to have fancied himself the Messiah and the Son of God; but instead of opposing all the popular notions, and discouraging all the temporal hopes, of his countrymen, he would, like Barcokeba of a later period, have headed a rebellion against the hated tyranny of the Romans, and endeavored to establish a temporal kingdom. Enthusiasm, which in this case must have bordered on madness itself, instead of calmly and patiently bearing the malignant opposition of the leaders of the nation, would have broken out in violent passion and precipitate action.

Christ's intellect is truly marvelous. He never erred in his judgment of men and things; he was never deceived by appearances; he penetrated through the surface, and always went straight to the heart and marrow; he never asked a question which was not perfectly appropriate; he never gave an answer which was not fully to the point, or which could be better conceived and expressed. How often did he silence his cavilers, the shrewd and cunning priests and scribes, by a short sentence which hit the nail on the head, or struck like lightning into their conscience, or wisely evaded the trap laid for him! When the Pharisees and Herodians, with the malicious intention to entangle him into their political party quarrels, asked him whether it was lawful to pay taxes to the Roman government, he, perceiving their wickedness, called for a penny with the superscription of the Roman emperor, and said: "Render unto Cæsar the things that are Cæsar's, and unto God the things that are God's,"—a word which settles, in, principle, the whole vexed question between Church and State, and which may be called the wisest answer ever given by any man. When the Sadducees, who denied the resurrection, laid before him a perplexing question concerning the marriage relation in the future state, he solved the difficulty by removing all foundation for it; and then, appealing to the very part of the Old Testament which they professed to believe to the exclusion of the later parts of the canon, he asked them: "Have ye not read that which was spoken unto you by God, saying, I am the God of Abraham, and the God of Isaac, and the God of Jacob? *God is not the God of the dead, but of the living.*" By this short comment he opened the profound meaning of this title of God, which no one had seen in it before, but which, being once brought to light, was so clear and transparent that even the Sadducees were silenced, and the multitude astonished. And when the sanctimonious hypocrites, in the case of the adulterous woman, hoped to involve him in a contradiction with the rigor of the law, he brought the matter home to their own conscience by saying: "He that is without sin among you, let him first cast a stone at her;" and they, "being convicted by their own conscience, went out one by one, beginning at the eldest, even unto the last." Christ never lost the balance of mind under excitement, nor the clearness of vision under embarrassment; he never violated the most perfect good taste in any of his sayings.

Is such an intellect—clear as the sky, bracing as the mountain air, sharp and penetrating as a sword, thoroughly healthy and vigorous, always ready and always self-possessed—liable to a radical and most serious delusion concerning his own character and mission? Preposterous imagination!

Let us hear the most eminent Unitarian divine on this hypothesis:—

"The charge," says Dr. Channing, "of an extravagant, self-deluding enthusiasm is the last to be fastened on Jesus. Where can we find the traces of it in his history? Do we detect them in the calm authority of his precepts; in the mild, practical, and beneficent spirit of his religion; in the unlabored simplicity of the language with which he unfolds his high powers and the sublime truths of religion; or in the good sense, the knowledge of human nature, which he always discovers in his estimate and treatment of the different classes of men with whom he acted? Do we discover this enthusiasm in the singular fact, that whilst he claimed power in the future world, and always turned men's minds to heaven, he never indulged his own imagination, or stimulated that of his disciples, by giving vivid pictures, or any minute description, of that unseen state? The truth is, that, remarkable as was the character of Jesus, it was distinguished by nothing more than by calmness and self-possession. This trait pervades his other excellences. How calm was his piety! Point me; if you can, to one vehement, passionate expression of his religious feelings. Does the Lord's Prayer breathe a feverish enthusiasm? . . . . His benevolence, too, though singularly earnest and deep, was composed and serene. He never lost the possession of himself in his sympathy with others; was never hurried into the impatient and rash enterprises of an enthusiastic philanthropy; but did good with the tranquillity and constancy which mark the providence of God."[1]

---

1. *"Discourse on the Character of Christ."*—Channing's *Works*, vol. iv. 17, 18.

4

THE RATIONALISTIC EXPLANATION.

PAULUS.

But the champions of this theory may admit all this, and yet fasten the delusion upon the *disciples* of Christ, who were so dazzled by his character, words, and works, that they mistook an extraordinary man for a divine being, and extraordinary medical cures for supernatural miracles.

This is the view of the older German Rationalism.[1] It forms a parallel to the heathen rationalism of Euhemerus, of the Cyrenaic school: he explained the gods of the Greek mythology as human sages, heroes, kings, and tyrants, whose superior knowledge or great deeds secured them divine honors, or the hero-worship of posterity.[2]

The rationalistic explanation, after having been tried first, by Eichhorn and others, with the miracles of the Old Testament, was fully developed and applied to the gospel-history, with an unusual degree of patient and painstaking learning and acumen, by the late professor H. E. G. Paulus, of Heidelberg.[3] This German Euhemerus takes the gospel-history as actual history; but, by a critical separation of what he calls *fact* from what he calls *judgment* of the actor or narrator, he explains it exclusively from natural causes, and thus brings it down to the level of everyday experience. In other words, the supernatural events related by the evangelists, and honestly believed by them, are erroneous conceptions and innocent amplifications of historical facts which fall within the sphere of the laws of nature. Sometimes the fault lies only in the reader or interpreter, and the supposed miracle turns out to be a grammatical blunder; as, for example, when Christ's walking ἐπὶ τῆς θαλάσσης (Matt. xiv. 25), which means simply his walking *on the bank* of the sea, or on the high *shore* above the sea,—a very easy and natural performance indeed!—is turned into a walking *on* the sea, or *over* the sea.[4]

This interpretation, however, which claims to be "natural," turns out to be very unnatural, and commits innumerable sins against the context, the laws of hermeneutics, and against common sense itself. To prove this, it is only necessary to give some specimens from the exegesis of Paulus and his school. The glory of the Lord, which, in the night of his birth, shone around the shepherds of Jerusalem, was simply an *ignis fatuus*, or a meteor, or a lantern which was flashed in their eyes. The miracle at Christ's baptism may be easily reduced to thunder and lightning, and a sudden disappearance of the clouds. The tempter in the wilderness was a cunning Pharisee, and was only mistaken by the evangelists for the devil, who does not exist, except in the imagination of the superstitious. The supposed miraculous cures of the Saviour turn out, on closer examination, to be simply deeds either of philanthropy, or medical skill, or good luck: thus the healing of the blind was accomplished through an efficacious powder applied to the eye,—a circumstance which was unnoticed by the miracle-loving reporters. The coin for the payment of tribute was to be obtained by Peter, not in *the mouth* of the fish, but by selling the fish in the market. The changing of water into wine was an innocent and benevolent wedding-joke; and the delusion of the company, by the sudden appearance of the wine previously provided by the disciples, must be charged on the twilight, not upon Christ. The miraculous feeding of the five thousand is easily explained by secret magazines, or by provisions which the people brought with them in their pockets,—Jesus, like a true philanthropist, advising the rich to share their abundance with the poor. The daughter of Jairus, the youth of Nain, Lazarus,. and Jesus himself, were raised, not from real death, but simply from a trance or swoon; and the angels of the resurrection were nothing more nor less than the white linen cloths which the pious mistook for celestial beings. And, finally, the ascension of the Lord resolves itself into his sudden disappearance behind a cloud that accidentally intervened between him and his disciples!

And yet these very evangelists, who, according to this most unnatural "natural exegesis," must have been destitute of the most ordinary talent of observation, and even of common sense, have contrived to paint a character and to write a story, which, in sublimity, grandeur, and interest, throws the productions of the proudest historians into the shade, and has exerted an irresistible charm upon Christendom for these eighteen hundred years! No wonder that those absurdities of a misguided learning and ingenuity hardly survived their author. It is a decided merit of Strauss, that he, in his larger work on the "Life of Jesus," has thoroughly refuted the system of his predecessor, and given it the critical death-blow. But his own theory will share no better fate. Renan too, in his "Essay on the Critical Historians of Jesus," speaks quite contemptuously of this "very narrow exegesis," this "shabby method of interpretation," "an exegesis made up of subtilties, founded on the mechanical use of a few incidents,—ecstasy, lightning, storm, cloud, etc.;" and says: "The so-called rationalistic interpretation may have satisfied the first bold desire of the human mind on its taking possession of a long-forbidden domain; but experience could not but disclose very soon the inexcusable defects, the dryness, the coarseness of it. Never was better realized the ingenious allegory of the daughters of Minos, who were turned into bats for having seriously criticised the vulgar credences. There is as much simplicity and credulity, and much less poetry, in clumsily discussing a legend in its details, as in accepting it, once for all, as it is."[5] So one infidel refutes the other, and by the very process undermines his own system.

---

1. The so-called *rationalismus communis*, or *vulgaris*, or the rationalism of common sense, as distinct from the transcendental rationalism of uncommon sense or speculative reason. The sense of both systems, however, ends in nonsense. Dr. Marheineke defined a Rationalist, or, as Paulus (not of Tarsus, but of Heidelberg) called him, a *Denkgläubige*, as a man, *der zu denken glaubt und zu glauben denkt; es ist aber mit beidem gleich null*; *i.e.*, a man who believes that he thinks, and

thinks that he believes; but both amounts to nothing. The Hegelian School has successfully ridiculed common or vulgar rationalism, and made every scholar of philosophical pretensions ashamed of it. But the infidel wing of that school has at last relapsed into the same or still greater absurdities.

2. Comp. Diodorus Siculus, *Bibli. Fragm.*, i. 7; Cicero, *De natura deor.*, i. 42; Sextus Empir., *Adv. math.* ix. 17.

3. Dr. Paulus was born in the kingdom of Württemberg, 1761; then successively professor in different universities; at last in Heidelberg, where he died in 1847, after having long outlived himself. His rationalistic exegesis is laid down in his *"Commentary on the Gospels,"* published since 1800; and in his *"Life of Jesus,"* 1828.

4. The rationalistic interpretation of περιπατῶν ἐπὶ τῆς θαλύσσης (according to the reading of the received text), or ἐπὶ τῆν θάλασσαν (according to the better authenticated reading of the modern critical editions), in Matt. xiv. 25, is perfectly inconsistent with the context and with the expression in verse 29, περιεπάτησεν ἐπὶ τὰ ὕδατα, and abandoned by all good commentators. It is true that the Greek preposition ἐπὶ with the *genitive* may mean, *on the bank of,* but only after verbs of *rest,* as in John xx., ἐπὶ τῆς θαλάσσης τῆς Τιβεριάδος, not after verbs of motion, as περιπατεῖν, and still less with the *accusative,* according to the proper reading of the oldest manuscripts.

5. Renan: *"Studies of Religious history and Criticism,"* translated by O. B. Frothingham. New York, 1864. pp. 176, 177.

5

THE THEORY OF POETICAL FICTION.

The last, the least dishonorable, and the most plausible, of the false theories of the life of Christ, is the hypothesis of poetical fiction. This may, again, assume two forms,—the *mythical* and the *legendary*. The former derives its support mainly from the formation of the ancient myths of heathen gods and demigods; the latter, from the medieval legends of Christian martyrs and saints.

The one was matured and carried out by Dr. David Frederick Strauss, with all the patient research, learning, and solidity of a German scholar; the other, by Prof. Joseph Ernest Renan, with all the brilliancy, elegance, and levity of a Parisian novelist: the one was written for students, the other for the people; the one rests on the philosophical basis of a speculative or logical pantheism, the other on that of a sentimental or poetical pantheism. Strauss's *"Leben Jesu"* is related to Renan's *"Vie de Jésus,"* as the heavy armor of a mediæval knight to the parade uniform of a holiday-soldier, or as a siege-cannon to a popgun, or as an iron statue to a tawdry wax figure; but both start essentially from the same naturalistic premises, and arrive at the same conclusions. They are equally opposed to the miraculous and supernatural in the life of our Saviour, and leave a mere spectral shadow, the *corpus mortuum,* of the real Jesus of the Gospels.

THE MYTHICAL HYPOTHESIS OF STRAUSS.

D r. Strauss wrote two works on the life of Jesus: a large one for scholars, which appeared first in 1835, in two volumes; and a condensed one for the people, in 1864, in one volume.[1] In both he maintains the same theory, with unimportant modifications. The former is no doubt the ablest and strongest work ever written against Christianity, and is at the same time a well-arranged storehouse of all the older arguments of infidelity in its attacks upon the gospel history. It is therefore worthy of a more serious examination and refutation than any other.

Strauss has found an eloquent advocate in the erratic genius and misguided philanthropist, Theodore Parker, who passed like a brilliant meteor over the American skies to disappear in a foreign land.[2]

What Gabler, Vater, Bauer, De Wette, and other critics, had already done with the miracles of the Old Testament, and some portions of the New, Strauss fully matured and carried out with reference to the whole life of Christ. He sinks the gospel history, as to the mode of its origin and realness, substantially on a par with the ancient mythologies of Greece and Rome.

A myth is the representation of a religious idea or truth in the form of a fictitious narrative; and in this respect it resembles the fable and the parable, but differs from both by blending the idea with the fact, without any consciousness of a difference between them. The fable is a fictitious story, based upon palpable impossibilities,—as thinking and speaking animals,—and invented for the express purpose of inculcating some moral maxim, or lesson of prudence; the parable is likewise a fictitious narrative, deliberately produced, but based upon possibilities, and thus intrinsically truthful, for the purpose of illustrating a spiritual truth; a myth is unconsciously produced, with the most simple and unreflecting faith in the actual occurrence of the story. The mytho-poetic faculty presupposes—and this we may remark, by way of antici-pation, is a very telling argument against the theory of Strauss—a childlike age of the human race, an entire absence of reflection and criticism. It works like the imagination of children, who delight in stories, invent stories, and believe their own stories without the least misgiving or doubt, without raising the question of truth or falsehood. In this way, according to the theory of some distinguished German scholars like Ottfried Müller, and English writers like Grote, the Greek mythology took its rise, as the spontaneous growth, or unconscious poem, of a child-like fancy, which peopled the air and the sea, the mountains and the groves, the trees and the brooks, with divinities, with the fullest belief in their actual existence. So, also, much of the legendary of mediæval Christianity can be accounted for; with the difference, however, that the legends of martyrs and saints have, in most cases, some foundation, not only in a psychological state, but also in some historical fact. The rest is either harmless poetry of simple souls, or pious fraud of monks and priests.

Strauss does not deny by any means, as is sometimes ignorantly or maliciously asserted, the historical existence of Jesus, and even admits him to have been a religious genius of the first magnitude. But from pantheistic and naturalistic premises, and by a cold process of hyper-critical dissection of the apparently contradictory accounts of the witnesses, he resolves all the supernatural and miraculous elements of Christ's person and history, from his birth to the resurrection and ascension, into myths, or imaginative representations of religious ideas in the form of facts, which were honestly believed by the authors to have actually occurred. The ideas symbolized in these facts, especially the idea of the essential unity of the divine and human, are declared to be true in the abstract, or as applied to humanity as a whole; but denied to be false in the concrete, or in their application to an individual. The authorship of the evangelical myths is ascribed to the primitive Christian community, pregnant with Jewish Messianic hopes, and kindled to hero-worship by the appearance of the extraordinary person of Jesus of Nazareth, whom they took to be the promised Messiah, and adorned with this innocent poetry of miracles within thirty or forty years after his death. The theory may be reduced to the following syllogism: There was a fixed idea in the Jewish mind, nourished by the Old Testament writings, that the Messiah would perform certain miracles,—heal the sick, raise the dead, &c.; there was a fixed persuasion in the minds of the disciples of Jesus that he actually was the promised Messiah: therefore the mytho-poetic faculty instinctively invented the miracles corresponding to the Messianic conception, and ascribed them to him.

In the execution of his task, Strauss avails himself, at the same time, of all the difficulties and objections which the ingenuity of unbelievers of opposite philosophical tendencies, from Celsus and Porphyry to Reimarus and Paulus, have urged against the credibility of the gospel narrative; grouping them with consummate skill for rhetorical effect; presenting the most complex details with rare clearness; changing his mode of attack from round assertion to cautious insinuation or suggestive inquiry, and then massing his forces for a final assault upon the citadel, against which the gates of hell shall never prevail.

Let us now proceed to examine this system.

First, The philosophic foundation on which the mythical hypothesis professedly rests is the alleged impossibility of a miracle; which, again, has its root in a pantheistic denial of a personal God and an Almighty Maker of heaven and earth. This fundamental principle, however, is a mere assumption, which the author never attempts to prove. His work, as to its philosophical groundwork, is a *petitio principii*, and begs the very question which it was one of its prime objects to discuss. Much as he boasted of possessing that freedom from doctrinal prepossessions (*dogmatische Voraussetzungslosigkeit*) as a first prerequisite for a scientific biography of Jesus, he starts with a stubborn prejudice. Moreover, he and Renan falsely assume that a miracle is necessarily a violation and suspension of the immutable laws of nature, and deranges the divinely appointed course of events. But a miracle is no such thing; it is simply a manifestation of a higher law; it is only above nature, not against nature. Bushnell, in his classical work on "Nature and the Supernatural," has conclusively shown, I think, that there is no more a suspension of the laws of nature, when God acts, than when man acts; since nature, by its very laws, is subject to God's and man's uses, to be swayed, modified, and made subservient to the higher kingdom. The laws of nature are not, as modern naturalists and materialists seem to suppose, iron chains by which the living God, so to say, is bound hand and feet, but elastic cords rather, which he can lengthen or shorten at his sovereign will.

Creation is the first miracle; and the Almighty Will, which called the world into existence, still lives with his power undiminished. God is the Lord of nature, and can reveal himself in his own realm. Geological discovery tells us, that, even before man, new races of animals and plants have at different times been created. The testimony of the rocks is full of such miracles. Mlan must have had a beginning,—even according to the pantheistic theory of development, if we trace it back in an unbroken line to the first link,—and he can not be explained from a lower kingdom, but only by a creative fact. As the plant is a miracle over against the stone, the animal over against the plant, so man is a miracle as compared with the irrational brute. In man himself, his intelligence is supernatural as compared with the body, and asserts its higher power continually over nature. If we raise our arm in obedience to our will, the law of gravity is held in temporary abeyance, or subordinated to the higher law of free action, but not abrogated or discontinued. Every virtue is a victory over nature, though not an annihilation of it. All this is no proper miracle, but it involves all the speculative difficulties of the miracle. If man can act upon nature from without, and control it, why not much more God, the independent Author and Executor of the laws of nature? Reasoning thus from analogy, we have a right to ascend to a higher sphere.

The belief in the supernatural, far from being a sign of a weak mind, has been held by intellectual giants among all nations and ages. St. Paul and St. John, Augustine and Chrysostom, Anselm and Thomas

Aquinas, Luther and Calvin, Bacon and Newton, Pascal and Guizot, Kepler and Leibnitz, Rothe and Lange, Edwards and Bushnell, are all arrayed here against Strauss and Renan, and have, to say the very least, furnished far stronger arguments in favor of the supernatural than these champions of modern naturalism have urged against it; for they merely oppose a modern *à-priori* assumption to a faith which is as old and universal as the race.

In the case of Christ, the presumption is altogether in favor of his having performed miracles; and the *onus probandi* lies on those who take the opposite view. Christ, we have seen, is himself a miracle, compared with all ordinary men before and after him. His doctrine and life not only rise far above his age and nation, but have never been surpassed or equaled since. Even Strauss, Renan, and Parker can not deny this fact, which is itself a miracle in the pantheistic development theory, so far as this requires a constant progress and improvement of the race. What else, then, can we expect from such a marvelous person, from the restorer of the race, the author of a new moral creation, the founder of a universal and everlasting kingdom of truth and right-eousness, but marvelous works, which are clearly established by the united evidence of his own testimony and that of all his disciples? To believe in Christ's person is to believe in his works, just as the belief in an Almighty God implies the belief in the creation, which is the first and great miracle and stumbling-block of naturalism. To deny the possibility of miracles is to deny the existence of a living God and Almighty Creator.

Secondly, The critical foundation of the mythical theory is as unsafe as the philosophical, and is one of the weakest parts of the book of Strauss, who was justly censured by his teacher, Baur, for attempting to write a criticism of the gospel history without a criticism of the Gospels. In order to avoid the necessity of supposing that Christ and the apostles were deceivers or self-deceived, and to allow a sufficient time for the formation of myths, he must bring down the canonical Gospels at least a century later than Christ. But at that time they were already universally acknowledged as canonical writings, and used in the Christian churches. Strauss has to encounter here the overwhelming mass of patristic testimonies in favor of the apostolic origin of these

Gospels, which far exceed in number and weight the testimony that can be brought to the support of any of the classical writers of Greece or Rome.

At one time, feeling the force of the unanimous voice of Christian antiquity and modern critical investigation, Strauss was disposed to admit the authenticity of the Gospel of John; but, seeing the fatal effect of this concession upon his conclusions, he soon after withdrew it, in the third edition of his large work.

But, since that time, the evidence in favor of John's authorship has only increased by the discovery of the *"Philosophumena"* of Hippolitus; from which it appears that the fourth Gospel was already used, even by the Gnostic heretics, in the early part of the second century. The whole controversy concerning the origin and character of the canonical Gospels, into which we can not here enter, has assumed half a dozen new phases since the first appearance of Strauss's book in 1835; so that this, in respect to the indispensable preliminary investigations of a scientific biography of Jesus, is quite out of date. As to the fourth Gospel, especially, the only alternative in the present stage of the controversy is truth or fraud. The assumption of unconscious mytho-poetical fiction is exploded by the latter developments of the Tübingen critics. Strauss himself now admits, in this case, conscious fiction and philosophical construction, and thus approaches the very border of the infamous theory of imposture.[3]

But suppose we give up the four Gospels: there still remain the Acts and the Epistles of the New Testament to substantiate all the fundamental facts of the life of Christ, especially the resurrection,—the great crowning and sealing miracle of his work, without which the Apostolic Church could never have risen at all. Even Dr. Baur, who, in bold negative and reconstructive criticism, went farther than any skeptic ever did, and who resolved most of the New-Testament writings into "tendency" books written in the conscious interest of contending parties and sections of the post-apostolic age, ultimately blended in the system of ancient Catholicism,—a theory, by the way, which is quite inconsistent with the unconscious mytho-poetic origin of the Gospels,—leaves the Apocalypse of St. John, and four Epistles of St. Paul, viz., those to the Romans (excepting the last two chapters), the Corinthians and Galatians, standing as genuine apostolic writings. This is enough for our purpose. It may perhaps be imagined that an illiterate fisherman of Galilee was simple and child-like enough to invent miracles, and to mistake the creatures of his fancy for actual facts. But this is a psychological impossibility in the case of Paul,—the learned, acute, subtle, dialectic, well-drilled rabbi of the school of Gamaliel, and so long the open and bitter enemy of Christianity. How could he submit his strong and clear mind, which was equal to that of any philosopher, ancient or modern, and devote all the energies of his noble life, which made him one of the greatest benefactors of mankind, to a poetical fiction, or empty dream of the very sect which he fanatically persecuted unto death?

The difficulty presented here to the infidel biographers of Jesus is absolutely insurmountable; and the chapter on the resurrection is the weakest part of Strauss's book, where his mythological hypothesis breaks down completely. He himself must admit that all the apostles believed in the resurrection, and could only by this belief pass from the despondency created by the death of Jesus, to the joy and enthusiasm necessary to spread the gospel and found churches at the risk of their lives. But he can not explain this astounding transition, which took place already on the third day. Rejecting the miracle, and also the natural interpretation of a resurrection from a trance, he resorts to a purely psychological resurrection of Christ in the visionary faith of his disciples, including St. Paul, and the more than five hundred to whom he appeared at once! (1 Cor. xv. 6.) As if an empty dream and unreal vision could suddenly turn desponding gloom into enthusiastic joy and world-conquering faith, and this in so many persons at the same time, and lay the foundation to the indestructible structure of the Christian Church! Credat Judæus Apella. Here, if anywhere, we must bow before the overwhelming force of a most glorious fact. Dr. Baur, the teacher of Strauss, and the acknowledged master of the modern critical school, felt the difficulty, and, toward the close of his long and earnest studies, honestly made the remarkable concession, that the conversion of Paul was to him a mystery, which could only be explained by "the miracle of the resurrection." [4] This concession overthrows the whole mythological fabric. Admit the resurrection of Christ, and there can be no difficulty with the other miracles.

A third fundamental error of the mythical hypothesis consists in a radical inversion of the natural order and relation of history and poetry, as it exists in any historical age like that in which Christ made his appearance on earth. Facts give rise to songs, and not *vice versâ*. Prophecies, and expectations, too, may foreshadow events, but do not create them. The real object precedes the picture of the artist; the hero, the epic. Bunyan's "Pilgrim's Progress" presupposes the Christian experience of which it is a beautiful allegory. Milton's "Paradise Lost" could never have produced the belief in the fall of man, but rests on this belief and the fact it describes with all the charm and splendor of sanctified genius. All the great revolutions in the world have been effected, not by fictitious personages, but by real living men whose power corresponded to their influence. So the American and French Revolutions in the eighteenth, the Puritan Revolution in the seventeenth, the Protestant Reformation in the sixteenth century; the founding of modern, mediaeval, and ancient empires; the inventions of arts, and the discoveries of new countries,—can all be traced to strictly historical and well-defined persons as originators or leaders. Why should Christianity, which produced the greatest of all moral revolutions of the race, form an exception? Ideas, without living men to represent and explain them, are shadows and abstractions. The pantheistic philosophy, on which the criticism of Strauss and Renan is based, by denying the personality of God, destroys also the proper significance of the personality of man, and consistently ends in denying the immortality of the soul.

In the case before us, the difficulty is greatly increased by making, not one great towering genius, as Homer, but an illiterate and comparatively ignorant multitude, responsible for the gospel poem, which in purity and sublimity rises infinitely above all ancient mythologies. Strauss assumes a Messianic community in some *terra incognita*, probably in the midst of Palestine, independent of the apostles, about thirty or forty years after the death of Christ, to have produced the gospel history. But this is a mere fiction of his brain. At that time, Christianity was already planted all over the Roman Empire, as is evident from the

Epistles of Paul as well as from the Acts; and all these congregations stood under the guidance of apostles and apostolic men who were eye-witnesses of the events of Christ, and controlled the whole Christian tradition. The Gospels, moreover, with the exception of that of Matthew, bear not the Jewish, but the Gentile-Christian stamp, and were written outside of Palestine, on Greek and Roman soil; which shows that the same traditions were spread all over the empire, and must form a part of the original Christianity of the apostles themselves. The mythological hypothesis breaks down half-way, and is forced to make the apostles responsible for the story; that is, to charge them with downright fraud. If Christ did not actually perform miracles, they must have been invented by the primitive disciples, the apostles, and evangelists, to account at all for their rapid and universal spread and acceptance among Jewish and Gentile Christians from Jerusalem to Rome.

But admitting such a consolidated, central, and yet independent mytho-poetic community of the second generation of Christians, how could this Messianic congregation itself originate without a Messiah? How could the disciples believe in Jesus, without the indispensable signs of the Messiahship? If the early Christians produced Christ, who produced the early Christians? Whence did they derive their high spiritual ideal? Were not the Messianic expectations of the Jews at the time sectional, political, and carnal,—the very reverse of those encouraged by Christ? Who ever heard of a poem unconsciously produced by a mixed multitude, and honestly mistaken by them all for actual history? How could the five hundred persons, to whom the risen Saviour is said to have appeared (1 Cor. xv. 6), dream the same dream at the same time, and then believe it as a veritable fact, at the risk of their lives? How could such an illusion stand the combined hostility of the Jewish and Heathen world, and the searching criticism of an age, not of child-like simplicity, but of high civilization, of critical reflection,—even of incredulity and skepticism? How strange, that unlettered and unskilled fishermen, or rather their obscure friends and pupils, and not the philosophers and poets of classic Greece and Rome, should have composed such a grand poem, and painted a character to whom Strauss himself is forced to assign the very first rank among all the religious geniuses and founders of religion! And would they not rather have given us at best an improved picture of such a rabbi as Hillel or Gamaliel, or of a prophet like Elijah or John the Baptist, instead of a universal reformer who rises above all the limitations of nation or sect?

The poets must in this case have been superior to the hero. John must have surpassed Jesus, whom he represented as the incarnate God.[5] And yet the hero is admitted by these skeptics themselves to be the purest and greatest man that ever lived!

But where are the traces of a fervid imagination and mytho-poetic art in the gospel history? Is it not, on the contrary, remarkably free from all rhetorical and poetical ornament, from every admixture of subjective notions and feelings, even from the expression of sympathy, admiration, and praise? The writers evidently felt that the story speaks best for itself, and could not be improved by the art and skill of man. Their discrepancies, which at best do not affect the picture of Christ's character in the least, but only the subordinate details of his history, prove the absence of collusion, attest the honesty of their intentions, and confirm the general credibility of their accounts. The Gospels have the character of originality and freshness stamped upon every page : they breathe the very presence of Jesus Christ; and this constitutes their irresistible charm to every unsophisticated reader. It is the history itself which speaks to us face to face, without intervening reflections and subjective notions. The few occasional references to geography, archaeology, and secular history, only confirm their general credibility. How different in all these respects the apocryphal Gospels! They are flat, puerile, insipid, the absurd productions of a diseased religious imagination. Here, indeed, we might speak of mythical or legendary fiction, or of downright imposition and pious fraud. But this very contrast proves the truth of the original. history, as the counterfeit implies the existence of the genuine coin.[6]

Verily, the gospel history, enacted not in an obscure corner (Acts xxvi. 26), but before the eyes of the people; before Pharisees and Sadducees; before Herod and Pilate; before Jews and Romans; friends and foes in Galilee, Samaria, and Judæa; a history related with such unmistakable honesty and simplicity by immediate witnesses and their pupils; proclaimed in open daylight from Jerusalem to Rome; believed by thousands of cotemporary Jews and Gentiles; sealed with the blood of apostles, evangelists, and saints of every grade of society and culture,—is better attested by external and internal evidence than any other history in the world.

The mere fact of the Christian Church, with its unbroken history of eighteen hundred years, is an overwhelming evidence of the Christ of the Gospels; and the institution of Christian baptism and the holy communion testify every day, all over the world, to the two fundamental doctrines of the holy Trinity, and of the atonement by the sacrifice on the cross. Strauss would make us believe in a stream without a fountain, in a house without a foundation, in an effect without a cause; for the facts which he and Renan leave untouched are not sufficient to account for the subsequent exaggerations and fictions, The same negative criticism which Strauss applied to the evangelists, would, with equal plausibility, destroy the strongest chain of evidence before a court of justice, and resolve the life of Socrates or Charlemagne or Luther or Napoleon into a mythical dream.[7]

But the secret spring of this hypercriticism is the pantheistic or atheistic denial of a personal, living God, which consistently and professedly ends with the denial of personal immortality; for the relative personality of man depends upon the self-conscious, self-existent, absolute personality of God. In its details, the mythical hypothesis is so complicated and artificial, that it can not be consistently carried out. It continually crosses the boundary-line which divides the mythical from the mendacious; and at the most critical points, as in the origin of the fourth Gospel and the miracle of the resurrection, it is driven to the alternative of admitting the truth, or relapsing to the vulgar and disreputable hypothesis of intentional fraud, from which it professed, at the start, to shrink back with horror and contempt.

---

1. David Friederich Strauss, Doctor of Philosophy (not of Theology), was born at Ludwigsburg, near Stuttgart, in Württemberg, a little kingdom which has produced an unusual number of distinguished men,—poets like Schiller and Uhland, philosophers like Schelling and Hegel, astronomers like Kepler, and some of the most orthodox and pious divines, as Bengel and Storr; but also the very leaders of both the common and the transcendental rationalism, viz. Paulus, Baur, and Strauss. The late Dr. Baur, Professor of Church History in Tübingen (died

1860), is the founder of the so-called Tübingen School of negative historical criticism, which aimed at a radical reconstruction of the history of primitive Christianity, on the basis of a pantheistic (Hegelian) intellectualism; and is, upon the whole, the ablest and most respectable of all the opponents of Christianity. It was mainly under his instruction that Strauss was educated. and unfitted for the Christian ministry, at the University of Tübingen.

He was the first in his class, and exhibited unusual talent and industry. After a literary journey to the north of Germany, he became *Repetent*, or theological tutor and lecturer, at the *Stift* (Seminary) of his Alma Mater; but was removed from this post and the service of the Church in 1836, after the publication of his famous "*Life of Jesus*," which created an extraordinary sensation in the theological and literary world, and gave him an unenviable notoriety for all time to come. Since that time, he has led a rather unsteady and apparently unhappy life in different places,—at Ludwigsburg, Stuttgart, Heilbronn, Weimar, Cologne, Munich, and again at Heilbronn. He married a famous actress, Agnese Schebest; but was shortly afterwards divorced from her, on account, not of immorality, but of incompatibility of temper, and of his extreme selfishness of disposition. In 1839, he was called to a professorship of didactic theology at the University of Zurich, but was prevented from taking possession of his chair by a revolution of the people of the canton, who stormed the city, and expelled the radical and infidel administration that called him to undermine the very foundations of the Christian faith in the rising ministry of the Church.

Strauss is a good classical and general scholar, and a master in the art of composition. He has a remarkably clear, methodical, logical, and acute mind, a rare power of critical analysis, but no constructive power whatever. He has talent of high order, but no genius; he can destroy, but not build up; he sees difficulties and differences, but no unity and harmony. He is an unscrupulous advocate and special pleader, who can tear the testimony of witnesses to pieces, but is unable to gain a positive result. In one word, he is a skillful "architect of ruin." As to his moral character, he is correct, temperate, and studious, but cold, selfish, and heartless. When a student, he was quite superstitious, and believed in all the ghost-stories and demoniacal possessions which then agitated Württemberg, and clustered around his friend, the amiable and humorous poet-physician and ghost-seer, Justinus Kerner of Weinsberg (who, by the way, called Strauss's marriage and subsequent divorce a mere "myth," and played many good-humored jokes on him). This is a striking illustration of the close affinity of superstition and infidelity, and the easy transition from one to the other. We have the same law exemplified on a large scale in the close alliance between infidelity and modern spiritualism falsely so called. Man must believe in something; either in the true God or in dumb idols, either in the Holy Ghost or in specters. Some time ago, it was currently reported in American papers that Strauss had changed his views, and was going to refute his "*Life of Jesus*;" but this dream is dissolved by the appearance of his new "*Life of Jesus*," which is as bad or even worse than the old.

The first and larger "*Leben Jesu*" of Strauss appeared at Tübingen in 1835 and '36, in two volumes; the fourth and probably the last edition in 1840; and was translated into French by Émile Littré, member of the Institute (Paris, 2d ed. 1856), and into English by Miss Marian Evans (London, 1846, in three volumes;

republished in New York by some obscure house, 1850). The smaller work under the same title, in one volume of 633 pages, appeared at Leipzig in 1864, and has already gone through several editions. While the first was intended exclusively for learned readers, the second is more popular (*für das deutsche Volk bearbeitet*, as the title-page says), and aims to be the same for the German people that Renan's "*Vie de Jésus*" was for the French, although it is as far behind the latter in easy elegance and popularity as it is above it in scholarship and accuracy. He dedicated it to the memory of his deceased brother, as Renan dedicated his work to the memory of his deceased sister. With slight modifications, he adheres to his old position, with increased bitterness to the clergy and the church, whom he now gives up hopelessly, turning to the people, and assuming the part of a theological deserter and spiritual demagogue. He has the impudence, in the preface (page 12), to appeal to the example of St. Paul, who, after being rejected by the Jews, offered the gospel to the Gentiles. He hopes that the annihilation of the popular faith in miracles will overthrow at last the Christian ministry, as a useless and even injurious encumbrance of society in the present advanced state of civilization. "*Wer die Pfaffen aus der Kirche schaffen will*," he says (preface, page 9), "*der muss erst das Wunder aus der Religion schaffern.*" The nature of the religion or philosophy which he would like to substitute for a supernatural Christianity may be judged from his undisguised denial of the immortality of the soul. He praises his deceased brother, in the words of dedication, for having never yielded, not even on his death-bed, to the deceitful temptation of deriving comfort from the empty dream of another world. "*Du hast*," he says, "*selbst in solchen Augenblicken, wo jede Lebenshoffnung erloschen war, niemals der Versuchung nachgegeben, durch Anlehnen beim Jenseits dich zu täuschen.*" Strauss has unwillingly done great service to the cause of truth by calling forth a library of learned defenses of the gospel history. Among his ablest opponents are Tholuck, Neander, Ullmann, Lamge, Ebrard, Jul. Muller, Hoffmann, Hug. Compare also a series of scholarly articles of Prof. Geo. P. Fisher of Yale College, on the "*Conflict with Skepticism and Unbelief*," the second of which reviews and refutes the mythical theory of Strauss, in the "*New-Englander*" for April, 1864. These articles, which appeared successively in the "*New-Englander*" and other American quarterly reviews, are well worth reprinting in permanent book form. In his new book, Strauss thinks it convenient to ignore almost entirely many of the best books bearing directly on the subject; as Tholuck's "*Credibility of the Gospel History*," Lange's "*Life of Christ*," and the masterly exegetical and critical labors of Meyer, Bleek, and others.

2. Theodore Parker, born in Massachusetts, 1810; died in Florence, 1860. "*Discourse of Matters pertaining to Religion*," 1849. Comp. his review of Strauss in the "*Christian Examiner*" for April, 1840. Mr. Weiss makes out a distinction between the theories of Strauss and Parker, but on a partial misapprehension of the former. The difference lies more in the practical turn of the American agitator and the speculative turn of the German student. See "*Life and Correspondence of Theodore Parker*," *by John Weiss*, New York, 1864, 2 vols.; and an able review of this work by Prof. Noah Porter in the "*New-Englander*" for 1864, page 359 ff.

3. In his new "*Leben Jesu*," page 79, Strauss says, with reference to the Gospel of John: "*Hier hat sogar die Einmischung philosophischer Construction und*

bewusster Dichtung alle Wahrscheinlichkeit." Comp. page 98. For a clear digest of the recent gospel controversy, we refer the English reader to two articles of Prof. G. B. Fisher in the "*Bibliotheca Sacra*" for April, 1864, on the genuineness of John; and another article in the "*New Englander*" for October, 1864, on the Synoptists.

4. Dr. Baur, in the second revised edition of his last important work on "*Christianity and the Christian Church in the First Three Centuries*," which appeared shortly before his death (a. 1860), makes the remarkable concession that the conversion of St. Paul remained at all times an enigma to him, which cannot be satisfactorily solved by any psychological or dialectical analysis. "*Keine weder psychologische noch dialektische Analyse kann das innere Geheimniss des Actes erforschen, in welchem Gott seinen Sohn in ihm enthüllte*" (p. 45). In this connection, he allows himself to speak of the *miracle* of the resurrection, "which alone could disperse the doubts of the older apostles, which seemed to doom faith itself to the eternal night of death" ("*das Wunder der Auferstehung, das allein die Zweifel der älteren Apostel zerstreuen konnte, welche den Glauben selbst in die ewige Nacht des Todes verstossen zu müssen schienen*" (p. 39); and of the *miracle* of Paul's conversion, which appears the greater, since he, "in the sudden change from the most violent enemy to the most determined herald of Christianity, broke through the barriers of Jewish particularism, and dissolved it in the universal idea of Christianity" (p. 45). We honor the honesty of this greatest of modern skeptics, and cherish the hope that he was saved at last from the eternal night of despair which is the legitimate end of skepticism.

5. The same objection against the theory of fiction was already raised by the infidel Rousseau, in his "*Émile*," L. iv. p. 111: "*Jamais des auteurs juifs n'eussent trouvé ni ce ton, ni cette morale; et l'évangile a des caractères de vérité si grands, si frappans, si parfaitement inimitable, que l'inventeur en serait plus étonnant que le héros.*" Theodore Parker, in arguing against the total denial of the existence of Jesus, which no sane man ever ventured upon, supplies an argument against the partial denial: "Measure Jesus by the shadow he has cast into the world; no, by the light he has shed upon it. Shall we be told such a man never lived? the whole story is a lie? Suppose that Plato and Newton never lived. But who did their works, and thought their thought? It takes a Newton to forge a Newton. What man could have fabricated a Jesus? None but a Jesus." Even Renan himself, unmindful of his theory, says, "*Life of Jesus*," ch. xxviii. p. 367: "Far from having been created by his disciples, Jesus appears in all things superior to his disciples. They, St. Paul and St. John excepted, were men without talent or genius. . . . Upon the whole, the character of Jesus, far from having been embellished by his biographers, has been belittled by them." What a pity that the world had to wait eighteen hundred years for a restoration of the true picture of Jesus from the imperfect and distorted fragments of his ignorant disciples!

6. Goethe, in his "Conversations with Eckermann" (vol. iii. 371), fully acknowledges the genuineness, credibility, and incomparable majesty of the Gospels, and says: "*Ich halte die Evangelien für durchaus ächt; denn est is in ihnen der Abglanz einer Hoheit wirksam, die von der Person Christi ausging und die so göttlicher Art, wie nur je auf Erden das Göttliche erschienen ist.*" Guizot, in his "*Méditations*," première série, p. 252, makes the following striking and truthful

remarks on the Gospels: "The mighty power of these books and their accounts has been tested and proved. They have overcome paganism; they have conquered Greece, Rome, and barbarous Europe; they are on the way of conquering the world. And the sincerity of the authors is no less certain than the power of the books. We may contest the learning and critical sagacity of the first historians of Jesus Christ; but it is impossible to contest their good faith; it shines from their words: they believed what they said; they sealed their assertions with their blood."

7. This has been done with good effect, with reference to Hume, by Archbishop Whately, in his "*Historic Doubts relative to Napoleon Bonaparte,*" Oxford, 1821; and against Strauss (which means Ostrich) by Dr. Wurm (under the name of *Casuar, i.e.* Cassowary, a cousin to the ostrich, not *Caspar*, as Prof. Fisher, in the "*New-Englander,*" 1864, p. 242, has it), in his "*Life of Luther,*" 1839, but dated Mexico, 1936 (not 2836), a hundred years after Strauss's "*Life of Jesus,*" when criticism shall have reached its climax in the New World. A very clever parody, which strictly follows the method of Strauss, and applies it to the documents relating to the life of Luther, which are often contradictory; for instance, as to his birthplace, Möhra, or Eisleben, or Mansfeld (compare Bethlehem and Nazareth), and the date and manner of his conversion at Erfurt, whether it was brought about by a duel, or by a thunder-storm and lightning, &c. Professor Norton, in his "*Internal Evidences of the Gospels,*" as we learn from Prof. Fisher, has likewise employed this weapon against Strauss, and by his own process conclusively proven that Julius Cæsar was never assassinated.

THE LEGENDARY HYPOTHESIS.

RENAN

This alternative is still more clearly forced upon us by the latest phase in the progress of infidelity,—the book of the Strauss of France.

Renan has eclipsed all former infidel biographers of Christ, so far as popularity and ephemeral effect is concerned. His "Life of Jesus," which first appeared in 1863, has had all the success of a sensation novel, and will probably share the same fate before it is ten years old.[1] In disposing of it, we can be much briefer, since a refutation of Strauss is also a refutation of Renan.

He essentially agrees, as already remarked, with Strauss, to whom he expressly refers as his main authority for critical research in detail; but he correctly remarks that the term *myths* is better applicable to India and primitive Greece than to the ancient traditions of the Hebrews and the Semitic nations in general; and prefers the words *legends* and *legendary narratives*, "which, while they concede a large influence to the working of opinions, allow the action and the personal character of Jesus to stand out in their completeness."[2] This brings the gospel history down to a level with the history of Francis of Assissi, and other marvelous saints of the Romish Church; although Renan, inconsistently enough, prefers a parallel between the myth of his favorite Cakya-Mouni, the founder of Buddhism, and the legend of Jesus, which again throws him back to the mythical theory.[3] He regards the so-called legend of Jesus as the fruit of consentaneous enthusiasm, and imaginative impulse of the primitive disciples. No great event in history has passed without a cycle of fables; and Jesus could not, had he wished, have silenced these popular creations.[4] He, moreover, differs from Strauss by admitting the essential authenticity of the chief portions of the four Gospels, including even the most contested of all, that of John,—a concession almost as fatal to his own as to the cognate mythical theory, and hence pronounced by Strauss the one essential error of Renan. He consequently allows a larger body of facts in the life of Christ. He undertakes, to some extent, the task of reconstruction, and proposes to clothe the cloudy phantom and dim shadow of the mythical Jesus with real flesh and blood. In his essay on the "Critical Historians of Jesus," he quotes with approbation the objection of Colani to Strauss: "No doubt the apostles, once believing in the Messianic character of Jesus, may have added to his actual image some lineaments borrowed from prophecy; but how came they to believe in his Messianic character? Strauss has never explained this. What he leaves of the Gospels is insufficient as ground for the apostles' faith; and it is useless to ascribe to them a disposition to be content with the minimum of proof: the proofs must needs have been very strong to overcome the crushing doubts occasioned by the death on the cross. In other words, the person of Jesus must have singularly surpassed ordinary proportions: a large part of the evangelical narratives must be true."[5] His "Life of Jesus" is, moreover, interspersed with truly eloquent and enthusiastic tributes to Jesus,—concessions which must either overthrow his whole legendary hypothesis, or else resolve themselves into empty declamation. So far, we may regard the French child as an improvement on its German parent, and a progress in the skeptical world towards the acknowledgment of the truth.

But while Renan, aided by clear common sense, a lively French imagination, and a fresh contemplation of the Holy Land, which he calls the "fifth Gospel," surpasses Strauss in the estimate of the historical character of the gospel-record, he is equally hostile to all miracles, which, in his oracular opinion, "always imply imposture or fraud;" and falls far below him on the score of scholarship, consistency, and even morality. We mean, of course, the morality of his theory, and have nothing to do with the morality of his life or private character. Compared with this critical master, Renan is a mere dilettante and a charlatan. He nowhere makes a serious attempt to prove any of his novel and arbitrary positions; refers for detail, once for all, to Strauss and half a dozen inferior infidel books; ignores their refutation, and the whole apologetic literature of the last thirty years; and deals in oracular assertions and eloquent declamations for artistic effect. His book nowhere rises to the dignity of solid science and scholarship. It is essentially a religious romance, with Jesus as the hero, adapted to the tastes of the fashionable world.[6]

According to Renan, Jesus was born at Nazareth (not at Bethlehem), but assumed the title of Son of David as a necessary condition of success. TIe grew up amidst the charming scenery of Galilee, an ignorant peasant of extraordinary genius and spotless virtue. He was a delicious Rabbi (Rabbi delicieux), of ravishing beauty, a preacher of the purest code of morals, and a healer of many diseases of body and mind. But finding at last that he had either to satisfy the foolish Messianic expectations of his people, or to renounce his mission, he yielded to his friends, and entered on a course of mild and beneficent deception. By a sudden and unaccountable transformation of character, this greatest man born of woman became a disappointed and morbid fanatic, a thaumaturgist, and a charlatan, who connived even at downright imposture and falsehood in the so-called resurrection of Lazarus, and paid for his error with his blood.[7] His life was at first a delightful pastoral and lovely idyl, at last a terrible tragedy, and ends for the historian with his expiring sigh on the cross. But so deep was the impression which this sublime though deluded genius and hero made, that he arose in the belief of his ignorant and credulous disciples. Thus the death of the man Jesus was the beginning of his worship as the incarnate God. The exact truth about the resurrection, Renan thinks, "on account of the contradictory documents," we shall never know, except that "the strong imagination of Mary Magdalene here enacted a chief part." "Divine power of love!" adds the enthusiastic declaimer; "sacred moments, when *the passion of a hallucinated woman* gave to the world a risen God!"[8]

And what a God!—such a God as only a heathen idolater, or a polluted fancy, or a crazy intellect, could worship; a Jesus who is idolized on the one hand as the perfect man, "whose legend will call forth tears without end, whose worship will grow young without ceasing;" and who almost in the same breath is charged with vanity, self-delusion, erotic sentimentalism, fanaticism, and complicity with fraud! We can hardly trust our eyes when we see this great Orientalist digging from the grave of disgrace and contempt the exploded hypothesis of vulgar imposture, as if it were the last conclusion of science; and read the suggestion that the resurrection of Lazarus was a pious fraud, contrived by himself and his two sisters, and weakly connived at by Jesus, in the hope of producing an impression among the unbelieving Jews. But this wretched opinion is, if possible, eclipsed by an entirely original invention of which neither Reimarus nor Paulus nor Strauss nor Celsus ever dreamed. Renan is not ashamed to outrage the feelings of all Christendom, and to disgrace himself, by profaning even the sacred agony in Gethsemane with the sensuous picture of a Parisian love-novel.[9] May God forgive him the criminal intrusion of such wanton fancies, from which every pious mind instinctively recoils in horror, as from a blasphemy of the Son of Man, and a direct approach to the unpardonable sin,—the blasphemy of the Holy Spirit! Much rather give up, with Strauss, the whole scene in the garden as unhistorical, than thus pollute and insult the suffering Redeemer, while bearing in boundless love the accumulated guilt of the whole race.

Renan's Jesus is the most contradictory and impossible character ever conceived. There are many happy and unhappy inconsistencies in the world, and even great and good men sometimes combine conflicting traits of character. But there is a great difference between inconsistencies and absolute contradictions; and not until all the laws of logic and psychology are overthrown, nor until fire and water, health and poison, dwell together in peace, will thinking, sensible people be made to believe that one and the same person can be a sentimentalist, an enthusiast, a fanatic, an impostor, a wise and charming rabbi, an unequaled saint, and an incarnate God. The Christ of the

Gospels requires faith; the Jesus of Renan, the utmost stretch of credulity. The Christ of history is a moral miracle; the Christ of romance, a moral monstrosity and an absurdity. Renan exposes himself to the combined force of the objections which have been urged in the preceding pages against all the false theories of the gospel history. His self-contradictory picture of Jesus, divested of the meretricious charms of a brilliant style and sentimental hero-worship, is an insult to sound sense and the dignity of man: it rouses the noblest instincts of our nature to just indignation, and is unworthy of a serious refutation. To state it in its nakedness is to expose, to refute, and to condemn it. Even as an artist he has failed in the main figure, since his hero lacks the essential quality of truthfulness of conception, unity and consistency of character; a defect arising not from any want of artistic power of representation, which we freely accord to him in an eminent degree, but from a sort of inevitable judgment which must overtake every one who dares, with unclean hands, to enter the *sanctissimum* of history, and to draw the picture of the purest of the pure and the holiest of the holy.[10]

---

1. Joseph Ernest Renan was born Feb. 27, 1823, at Treguier in Brittany, of humble (some say of Jewish) parents, and educated for the Romish priesthood in the Theological Seminary of St. Sulpice, at Paris. But, before taking orders, he was compelled to leave this institution on account of some religious difficulties which his superiors were unable or unwilling to solve. He then devoted himself to the comparative study of the Semitic languages, for which he endeavored to do what Prof. Bopp of Berlin had so successfully accomplished for the Indo-Germanic or Aryan family of languages. In 1847, he gained the Volney Prize for an essay, since expanded into a history of the Semitic languages, and acquired the reputation of one of the first living Orientalists of Europe. In 1856, he was elected (in place of Augustin Thierry) a member of the Institute of France. In 1860, he was intrusted by Napoleon III. with a mission for archaeological explorations on the supposed sites of the Phoenician cities, and published the results of his investigations in an ample collection of epigraphic monuments from the time of the Assyrian domination to that of the Seleucides. On his return, he was appointed to the professorship of Hebrew in the College of France, but lost his position in consequence of his inaugural address, in which he boldly attacked, in the name of free science, the traditional orthodoxy of the clerical party, and the venerable dogma of the divinity of Christ.

   Renan's "*Vie de Jésus*" was prepared, as to its outline, during his journey in the East, at the side of his since departed sister, in fresh view of the holy places, and published at Paris in 1863, as the first part of a work (to be finished in four volumes) on the *"Origins of Christianity."* It marks an epoch in the religious literature of France, and found an unparalleled circulation on the continent of Europe, and even i! England and America. I have before me the seventh edition, Paris, 1864. An English translation, by *Ch. E. Wilbour*, appeared in New York, 1864. The book of Renan has all the charm of a religious novel, and may have benefited many Frenchmen, who never knew that Jesus was such an interesting character, by inducing them to study the New Testament. So good will no doubt come out of evil also in this case. But, as a critical or scientific work, it has no value whatever. In the introduction, he refers, among six works, mainly to the *"Life of Jesus"* by Strauss, as translated by Littré, for information in critical details; and contents himself with stating his views with oracular self-assurance, and a show of indiscriminate references to the New. Testament and the Talmud, several of which prove the very reverse of the assertions in the text. Of the many refutations of Strauss he says not a word. He published also a smaller edition of his *"Life of Jesus,"* presenting him, as he; says, in "pure white marble" (in sugar-candy rather), without spot or wrinkle, for the edification of the French people. Among the many replies to Renan, I mention those of E. de Pressensé of France, Van Oosterzee of Holland, Beyschlag of Germany, and H. B. Smith of the United States.

2. See Renan's essay on the *"Critical Historians of Jesus,"* in his *"Studies of Religious History and Criticism,"* translated by O. B. Frothinghan, New York, 1864, p. 189.

3. In the essay just quoted, p. 197, Renan says: "The legend of the Buddha Cakya-Mouni is the one which, in its mode of formation, most resembles that of Christ; as Buddhism is the religion which, in the law of its development, most resembles Christianity." The mere fact of the comparative obscurity of this fellow, Cakya-Mouni, in the civilized world, makes the repeated comparison of Jesus with him by this French novelist simply ridiculous, if not blasphemous.

4. *"Vie de Jésus"* (ch. xv. p. 172): *"La légende était ainsi le fruit d'une grande conspiration toute spontanée et s'élaborait autour de lui de son vivant. Aucun grand événement de l'histoire ne s'est passé sans donner lieu à un cycle de fables, et Jésus n'eût pu, quand il l'eût voulu, couper court à ces créations populaires."*

5. *"Studies of Religious History and Criticism,"* &c., p. 192.

6. All competent judges seem to agree in a very low estimate of the scientific and critical value of Renan's book. Dr. H. B. Smith of New York, in his excellent review of Renan's *"Life of Jesus,"* in the *"American Presbyterian and Theological Review"* for January, 1864, p. 145, justly remarks: "In point of learning, intellect, and consistency, the Teutonic work of Strauss is immeasurably superior to the light and airy French romance." Prof. Fisher expresses the same opinion in the article already quoted, *"New Englander"* for 1854, p. 264: "There is nothing formidable in Renan's attack upon Christianity. It is too unscientific in its whole method to make a lasting impression. In comparison with the work of Strauss, it is of little account; and we doubt not that the ultimate effect of the commotion it has excited, and of the examination it must undergo, will be to exhibit more impressively than ever the difficulty of overthrowing the proofs of revelation." The Rev.

Marcus Dods, in the preface to the Edinburgh translation of Lange's "*Life of Christ*," vol. i. p. xiv., calls Renan's book "the most deplorable literary mistake of this century," and remarks that it reveals a lamentable ignorance on the part of the French public, that a book, which in Germany would have been out of date twenty years ago, should now create so much excited interest. The Rev. Samuel J. Andrews, in the preface to a new edition of his unpretending, but judicious, careful, and reliable "*Life of our Lord upon Earth*," New York, 1864, p. vi., denies to Renan's book all critical value, and adds: "I do not recall any particular in which it adds any thing to our knowledge of the gospel history, even in its external features: much less does it render us any aid in the understanding of its higher meaning."

7. "Jesus was a thaumaturgist only at a late period, and against his will." "He was a miracle-worker and an exorcist only in spite of himself. Miracles are ordinarily the work of the public even more than of him to whom they are attributed. . . . The miracles of Jesus were a violence done him by his time, a concession which the necessity of the hour wrung from him. So the exorcist and the miracle-worker have fallen; but the religious reformer, shall live for ever" (Renan, ch. xvi.). "Desperate, pushed to extremities, he no longer retained possession of himself. His mission imposed itself upon him, and he obeyed the torrent. As always happens in great and divine careers, he suffered the miracles which public opinion demanded of him, rather than performed them. Thoroughly persuaded that Jesus was a worker of miracles, *Lazarus and his two sisters may have aided in the performance of one* [the apparent resurrection of Lazarus], as so many pious men, convinced of the truth of their religion, have sought to triumph over human obstinacy by means of the weakness of which they were well aware. The state of their conscience was that of the Stigmatists, the Convulsionists, the Observed Nuns, led on by the influence of the world in which they live, and by their own belief in the pretended acts. As to Jesus, he had no more power than St. Bernard or St. Francis d'Assisi to moderate the avidity of the multitude and of his own disciples for the marvellous. Death, moreover, was in a few days to restore to him his divine liberty, and to snatch him from the fatal necessities of a character which became each day more exacting, more difficult to sustain" (chap. xxii.). So Jesus lent himself an instrument to a pious fraud. Of course, it would not be in keeping with French politeness or ordinary prudence to say, in plump terms, that Christ was an impostor; but the insinuation is clear enough for any reflecting reader.

8. At the close of chap. xxvi. (page 308 of the French original): "*Son corps avait-il été enlevé, ou bien l'enthusiasme, toujours crédule fît-il éclore après coup l'ensemble de récits par lesquels on chercha à établir la foi à la resurrection? C'est ce que, faute de documents contradictories*—[which the American translation, page 357, has softened into, 'for want of peremptory evidence']—*nous ignorerons à jamais. Disons cependant que la forte imagination de Marie de Magdala joua dans cette circonstance un rôle capital. Pouvoir divin de l'amour! moments sacrés où la passion d'une hallucinée donne au monde un Dieu ressuscité!*"

9. The reader will hardly believe it, until he reads the passage in "*Vie de Jésus*," chap. xxiii., which we reluctantly copy: "Did he [Christ in Gethsemane] recall the clear fountains of Galilee where he might have refreshed himself; the vineyard and fig-tree under which he might have been seated; *les jeunes filles qui auraient*

peut-être consenti à l'aimer? Maudit-il son âpre destinée, qui lui avait interdit les joies concédées à tous les autres? Regrettat-il sa trop haute nature, et, victime de sa grandeur, pleura-t-il de n'être pas resté un simple artisan de Nazareth?" Renan most arbitrarily places the scene in Gethsemane several days before the night of the passion, contrary to the unanimous testimony of the Synoptical Gospels as well as the inherent probability of the case. But the opinions of this frivolous critic on such subjects are worth nothing at all. The maidens of Galilee and Judea figure prominently in this novel of Jesus, and make it the more palatable to French taste. In chap. v. (page 52 of the original, page 102 of the English translation) occurs the following passage: "All his power to love was transferred to what he considered his celestial vocation. The extremely delicate feeling (*le sentiment extrêmement délicat*) which we notice in him towards women never departed from the exclusive devotion which he had to his idea. He treated as sisters, like Francis d'Assisi and Francis de Sales, those women who were enamored with the same work as he: he had his St. Claires, his Françoises de Chantal. Only it is probable that they loved him more than the work. He was undoubtedly more loved than loving. As often happens in very lofty natures, tenderness of heart was in him transformed into an infinite sweetness, a vague poetry, a universal charm. His relations, intimate and free, but of an entirely moral order, with women of equivocal conduct (*avec des femmes d'une conduite équivoque*), are explained also by the passion which attached him to the glory of his Father, and inspired in him a kind of jealousy of all beautiful creatures (*une sorte de jalousie pour toutes les belles créatures*) who might contribute to it." In proof of this reckless and frivolous talk, Renan quotes Luke vii. 37; John iv. 7; viii. 3. Guizot, no doubt with reference to Renan, devotes a special chapter of his *Méditations* to *Jésus-Christ et les femmes* (p. 309 if.), and justly maintains that nowhere is there less of man, and more of the God, than in Christ's relations with the women who approach him, and in the absolute purity which characterizes his sayings on adultery and on the sanctity of the marriage relation. Comp. Matt. v. 27, 28; xix. 4-9, etc.

10. Dr. H. B. Smith, in the article alluded to, pages 157 and 169, thus severely but justly condemns the book of Renan: "In passing judgment on such a representation, there is no need of circumlocution or euphonisms. It is utterly disgraceful and disingenuous. It assails the very honesty and credibility of Jesus. It makes success the standard. It is the essence of Jesuitism. The apology is as superficial as it is ignominious. The worst ethics of the French stage cannot surpass it. Nobody but a Frenchman could, after this, still idolize his hero as the perfection of humanity. And, in the midst of such profligate representations, to interject phrases about '*our* profound seriousness,' 'rigid conscience,' and 'absolute sincerity,' in contrast with the delusions and falsity attributed to Jesus, is to carry to its hight a base invention, from which every right-minded man will instinctively recoil, and which every true believer in Christ will stamp as blasphemy. Better for Jesus,—as a mere man,—a thousand-fold better, to have died unknown, than to have lent himself to impostures which he must have known to be false, to a conspiracy founded on a lie or a hallucination. But this is not all, nor the worst. The part of the Messiah made it necessary that Jesus should also give himself forth as an 'exorcist and a thaumaturge.' Charlatanry must complete the work begun in hallucination. . . . The Jesus depicted by Renan is a figment of natural-

ism, a conception that can neither be imaged forth nor realized. It has the outward forms and framework of human life; but within there is not even an immortal personal consciousness. We have, in the last analysis, only the shadow of death. And here is the essence of naturalism. The Jesus of the Gospels, of the Epistles, and of the Church, is human and divine, is king and priest in an eternal kingdom, is the essence of supernaturalismn; and naturalism must expel Christ from the heart and the church, from the conscience and the life, before it can expel supernaturalism from human history."

CONCLUSION

NEBICULA *est; transibit*,"—"It is a little cloud; it will pass away." This was said first, I believe, by Athanasius, of Julian the Apostate who, after a short reign of intense hostility to Christianity, perished with his work, "leaving no wreck behind."[1] The same may be applied to all the recent attempts to undermine the faith of humanity in the person of its divine Lord and Saviour. The clouds, great and small, pass away; the sun continues to shine: darkness has its hour; the light is eternal. No argument against the existence or attack upon the character of the sun will drive the king of day from the sky, or prevent him from blessing the earth. And the eye of man, with its sun-like nature, will ever turn to the sun, and drink the rays of light as they emanate from the face of Jesus, the "Light of the world." "God, who commanded the light to shine out of darkness, hath shined in our hearts to give the light of the knowledge of the glory of God in the face of Jesus Christ" (2 Cor. iv. 4).

With its last and ablest efforts, infidelity seems to have exhausted its scientific resources. It could only repeat itself hereafter. Its different theories have all been tried, and found wanting. One has in turn refuted and superseded the other, even during the lifetime of their champions. They explain nothing in the end: on the contrary, they only substitute an unnatural prodigy for a supernatural miracle, an inextricable enigma for a revealed mystery. They equally tend to undermine all faith in God's providence, in history, and ultimately in every principle of truth and virtue; and they deprive a poor and fallen humanity, in a world of sin, temptation, and sorrow, of its only hope and comfort in life and in death.

Dr. Strauss, by far the clearest and strongest of all the infidel biographers of Jesus, seems to have had a passing feeling of the disastrous tendency of his work of destruction, and the awful responsibility he assumed. "The results of our inquiry," he says in the closing chapter of his large "Life of Jesus," "have apparently annihilated the greatest and most important part of that which the Christian has been wont to believe concerning his Jesus; have uprooted all the encouragements which he has derived from his faith, and deprived him of all his consolations. The boundless stores of truth and life which for eighteen hundred years have been the aliment of humanity seem irretrievably devastated, the most sublime leveled with the dust, God divested of his grace, man of his dignity, and the tie between heaven and earth broken. Piety turns away with horror from so fearful an act of desecration, and, strong in the impregnable self-evidence of its faith, boldly pronounces that—let an audacious criticism attempt what it will—all that the Scriptures declare and the Church believes of Christ will still subsist as eternal truth; nor need one iota of it be renounced."[2] Strauss makes then an attempt, it is true, at a philosophical reconstruction of what he vainly imagines to have annihilated as an historical fact by his sophistical criticism. He professes to admit the abstract truth of the orthodox Christology, or the union of the divine and human, but perverts it into a purely intellectual and pantheistic meaning. He refuses divine attributes and honors to the glorious Head of the race, but applies them to a decapitated humanity. He thus substitutes, from pantheistic prejudice, a metaphysical abstraction for a living reality; a mere notion for an historical fact; a progress in philosophy and mechanical arts for the moral victory over sin and death; a pantheistic hero-worship, or self-adoration of a fallen race, for the worship of the only true and living God; the gift of a stone for the nourishing bread; a gospel of despair and final annihilation, for the gospel of hope and eternal life.[3]

Humanity scorns such a miserable substitute, which has yet to give the first proof of any power for good, and which is not likely ever to convert or improve a single individual. Humanity must have a living Head, a real Lord, and Saviour from sin and death. With renewed faith and stronger confidence, it will return from the dreary desolations of a heartless infidelity, and the vain conceits of a philosophy falsely so called, to the historical Christ, the promised Messiah, the God incarnate, and exclaim with Peter: "Lord, where shall we go but to thee? Thou alone hast the words of eternal life, and we believe and are sure that thou art the Son of God!"

Yes! He still lives, the divine Man and incarnate God, on the ever-fresh and self-authenticating records of the Gospels, in the unbroken history of eighteen centuries, and in the hearts and lives of the wisest and best of our race; and there he will live for ever. His person and work are the book of life, which will never grow old. Christianity lives and will continue to live with him, and because he lives, the same yesterday, to-day, and for ever.

Jesus Christ is the most certain, the most sacred, and the most glorious, of all facts; arrayed in a beauty and majesty which throws the "starry heavens above us and the moral law within us" into obscurity, and fills us truly with ever-growing reverence and awe. He shines forth with the self-evidencing light of the noonday sun. He is too great, too pure, too perfect, to have been invented by any sinful and erring man. His character and claims are confirmed by the sublimest doctrine, the purest ethics, the mightiest miracles, the grandest spiritual kingdom, and are daily and hourly exhibited in the virtues and graces of all who yield to the regenerating and sanctifying power of his spirit and example. The historical Christ meets and satisfies all our intellectual and moral wants. The soul, if left to its noblest impulses and aspirations, instinctively turns to him, as the needle to the magnet, as the flower to the sun, as the panting hart to the fresh fountain. We are made for him, and "our heart is without rest until it rests in him." He commands our assent, he wins our admiration, he overwhelms us with adoring wonder. We can not look upon him without spiritual benefit. We can not think of him without being elevated above all that is low and mean, and encouraged to all that is good and noble. The very hem of his garment is healing to the touch. One hour spent in his communion outweighs all the pleasures of sin. He is the most precious and indispensable gift of a merciful God to a fallen world. In him are the treasures of true wisdom, in him the fountain of pardon and peace, in him the only substantial hope and comfort in this world and that which is to come. Mankind could better afford to lose the whole literature of Greece and Rome, of Germany and France, of England and America, than the story of Jesus of Nazareth. Without him, history is a dreary waste, an inextricable enigma, a chaos of facts without a meaning, connection, and aim: with him, it is a beautiful, harmonious revelation of God, the slow but sure unfolding of a plan of infinite wisdom and love.; all ancient history converging to his coming, all modern history receiving from him its higher life and impulse. He is the glory of the past, the life of the present, the hope of the future. We can not even understand ourselves without him. According to an old Jewish proverb: "The secret of man is the secret of the Messiah." He is the great central Light of history, as a whole; and, at the same time, the Light of every soul: he alone can solve the mystery of our being, and fulfill all our intellectual desires after truth, all our moral aspirations after goodness and holiness, and the longing of our feelings after peace and happiness.

Not for all the wealth and wisdom of this world would I weaken the faith of the humblest Christian in his divine Lord and Saviour; but if, by the grace of God, I could convert a single skeptic to a child-like faith in Him who lived and died for me and for all, I would feel that I had not lived in vain.

---

1. The dying exclamation of Julian the Apostate—"Galilæan, thou hast conquered!"—rests on too late authorities to claim credibility, especially in view of the full account of the impartial Ammianus Marcellinus on the last hours of the emperor. But it contains the philosophy of his reign, and the Italian proverb may be applied to it: *Se non e vero, e ben trovato.*
2. See his large "*Leben Jesu,*" Schlussabhandlung, vol. ii. page 663 (4th ed., 1840). Compare a similar conclusion in his popular "*Leben Jesu,*" page 627.
3. "In an individual," says Strauss, "*Leben Jesu,*" vol. ii. page 710, "in one God-man, the properties and functions which the church doctrine ascribes to Christ contradict themselves; in the idea of the race, they agree. *Humanity* is the union of the two natures,—the incarnate God, the Infinite externalizing itself in the finite,

and the finite spirit remembering its infinitude. It is the child of the visible mother and the invisible father, Nature and Spirit; it is the worker of miracles, in so far as in the course of human history the spirit more and more completely subjugates nature both within and around man, until it lies before him as an inert matter of his activity; it is the sinless existence, for the course of its development is a blameless one: pollution cleaves to the individual only, and does not touch the race or its history. It is humanity that dies, rises, and ascends to heaven: for from the negation of its natural life there ever proceeds a higher spiritual life;' from the suppression of its limitation as a personal, rational, and terrestrial spirit, arises its union with the infinite Spirit of the heavens. By faith in this Christ, especially in his death and resurrection, man is justified before God; that is, by the kindling within him of the idea of humanity, especially by the negation of its natural and sensual aspects, the individual man partakes of the divinely human life of the species." The popular "*Life of Jesus*," by the same author, concludes in a similar manner, page 627. But the idea of the union of the human and divine is no more contradictory in an individual than in the race. What is true in idea or principle must also actualize itself, or be capable of actualization, in a concrete living fact. History teaches, moreover, that every age, every great movement, and every nation, have their representative heads, who comprehend and act out the life of the respective whole. Compare the remarks on page 77 ff. This analogy points us to a general representative head of the entire race,—Adam in the natural, and Christ in the spiritual order. The divine humanity of Strauss is like a stream without a fountain, or like a body without a head.

POSTSCRIPT

In his latest book,—*The Christ of Faith and the Jesus of History*, Berlin, 1865,—which may be regarded as an Appendix to his second *Life of Jesus*, Strauss repeats, without proof, the same objection to the universal faith of the Christian Church: viz., that Jesus can not have been both a true man and a perfect superhuman being; in other words, that personality necessarily implies limitation and defect. This work presents no new features, but ably exposes the. fallacies of compromises between truth and error, and so far unwillingly serves the cause of truth. It is a clear and acute analysis of the posthumous Lectures of Schleiermacher on the *Life of Jesus*, with a sarcastic appendix against Schenkel's *Charakter-Bild Jesu*. Schleiermacher was a supernaturalist in Christology and a rationalist in exegesis, combining personal faith in Christ as his Saviour with the boldest criticism of the gospel history. Strauss vainly imagines that the failure of this last attempt to reconcile the old faith with modern philosophy and criticism must be disastrous to Christianity; as if this depended on Schleiermacher or any other man, or number of men! The whole issue raised by Strauss in the title of his book is false. The Christ of faith is the Jesus of history, and has stood the test of centuries; but the Jesus of rationalism and pantheism is a modern fiction, which will soon take its place among the exploded errors and follies of the human mind.

Also Available

THE HISTORICAL JESUS
AND MYTHICAL CHRIST